The Intersection of Poetry and Jungian Analysis Through Metaphor

The Intersection of Poetry and Jungian Analysis Through Metaphor

In Creation You Are Created

Regina Colonia-Willner

LEXINGTON BOOKS
Lanham • Boulder • New York • London

Published by Lexington Books
An imprint of The Rowman & Littlefield Publishing Group, Inc.
4501 Forbes Boulevard, Suite 200, Lanham, Maryland 20706
www.rowman.com

86-90 Paul Street, London EC2A 4NE

British Library Cataloguing in Publication Information Available

Library of Congress Cataloging-in-Publication Data

Names: Colônia-Willner, Regina (Regina Célia), author.
Title: The intersection of poetry and Jungian analysis through metaphor : in creation you are created / Regina Colonia-Willner.
Description: Lanham : Lexington Books, 2024. | Originally presented as author's thesis--C.G. Jung-Institut, Zurich, Switzerland. | Includes bibliographical references and index.
Identifiers: LCCN 2024024903 (print) | LCCN 2024024904 (ebook) | ISBN 9781666944457 (cloth) | ISBN 9781666944464 (ebook)
Subjects: LCSH: Metaphor--Psychological aspects. | Poetry--Psychological aspects. | Jungian psychology.
Classification: LCC PN228.M4 C59 2024 (print) | LCC PN228.M4 (ebook) | DDC 808.101/9--dc23/eng/20240609
LC record available at https://lccn.loc.gov/2024024903
LC ebook record available at https://lccn.loc.gov/2024024904

To Erich and Romulo

Contents

Preface

This book explores the relationship between poetry and Jungian psychoanalytical intervention, focusing on the emergence of metaphor, which occurs in both processes—as it also occurs in neuroscience and fairy tales, where associative linkages are present. Metaphor is a mode of communication that forms a bridge between different experience domains through associative linkages: it refers to one thing by mentioning another for rhetorical effect. Simile, metonymy, antithesis, and hyperbole are all types of metaphors. They can add meaning, emotion, and surprising clarification to developing a poem or a fairy tale and unearthing unconscious content when working with a client's individuation. The occurrence of metaphor will be studied in this book, both from the literary and the psychoanalytic perspectives.

Jung was interested in poetry and the arts as opportunities to explore archetypal dimensions. He famously stated that "In creation, you are created." This paper aims to develop our capacity to use language in our creative function in its "full richness, complexity and movement of living a human experience," as the psychoanalyst Thomas Ogden proposed in *The Music of What Happens in Poetry and Psychoanalysis.*[1] We will also have the opportunity to recall Wisława Szymborska, the Nobel laureate in poetry, who contends that "Poetry is the operative exercise of not knowing."[2] This could remind us of Jung considering his initial attempt to interpret a dream and asserting that "I have no idea what this dream is about."[3] The great poet and the gifted analyst work deeply in the unconscious through metaphor.

A noteworthy direction in the recent history of the analytical process and the creation of poetry has shown increased awareness toward how effects created in language—meaning what language *does* "alongside and beyond" what it *says*—bring essential contributions to the revelation of unconscious content. The study of metaphor constitutes a fundamental example of that direction.

This book explores the relationship between poetry and Jungian psychoanalytical practice, focusing on the emergence of metaphor in both processes.

Indeed, the prominence of metaphor in Jungian therapy is a characteristic that differentiates it from other forms of psychological treatment. That's because metaphor—as we will see in this book—is deep-rooted in the body in two ways: it is used to organize bodily sensations cognitively, mainly affects, and additionally, metaphor is rooted in the body because it is located on the border between mind and brain.

This is a multidisciplinary book, original, rich, thought-provoking, and scientifically based.

Special is the connection of the intellectual approach, the discussion of many authors, the study of groundbreaking foundational discoveries in neuroscience, and the innovative, cutting-edge analytical practice with detailed case studies empowered by the incorporation of poems.

The author's work as a psychoanalyst, poet, and scientist has been published internationally. Colonia-Willner has received significant honors and awards in the topics covered by this book, built an international readership, and collaborated with different groups and societies for speaking engagements, class lectures, and course adoption.

Metaphor, the book's encompassing subject area, is widely researched, as demonstrated in breakthrough neuroscience research, psychoanalysis, and poetry—and studied in fulfilling, practical ways throughout the book.

The prominence of metaphor in Jungian therapy is a characteristic that differentiates analytical psychology from other forms of psychological treatment.

That's because metaphor—as we will see in this book—is deep-rooted in the body in two ways: it is used to organize bodily sensations cognitively, mainly affects, and additionally, metaphor is rooted in the body because it is located on the border between mind and brain.

The book explores the relationship between poetry and Jungian psychoanalytical practice, focusing on the emergence of metaphor in both processes. Metaphor is a communication mode that bridges different experience domains through associative linkages: it refers to one thing by mentioning another for rhetorical effect. Simile, metonymy, antithesis, and hyperbole are all types of metaphors. They can add meaning, emotion, and surprising clarification to the development of a poem and the process of unearthing valuable unconscious content in working with a client's psychological process of individuation.

The occurrence of metaphor is presented in this book, both from the poet's and the psychoanalyst's perspectives, enriching it with the study of its foundation in state-of-the-art neuroscience research, experiencing it from contemporary multiple vivid poems and adding throughout its chapters illuminating client's cases examples.

This research will appeal to psychologists, psychoanalysts, neuroscientists, poets, professors of literature, and readers with an invested interest in literature. In addition, the book will appeal to professionals in other areas: coaches, mentors, human resources, management professionals, and artists. The book will be invaluable to anyone who wants to understand communication.

The idea of wholeness is at the etymological root of both healing and health. To heal, then, is to take what has been broken, separated, fragmented, injured, exiled, and restore it to wholeness," writes the American poet Jane Hirshfield in her essay "Poetry, Permeability, and Healing."[4]

If we think of something in our life that has been either physically or figuratively broken, fragmented, or made distant, writing a poem, or immersing ourselves in a vivid one attempts to find a way to restore its wholeness. This is like what happens in an analytical session, especially if it is a Jungian analytic session. In both experiences, a decisive key is represented by metaphor.

In fact, Antal F. Borbely, in "A Psychoanalytic Concept of Metaphor"—published in the *International Journal of Psycho-Analysis* (1998), suggests that the concept of metaphor belongs neither exclusively to the linguists nor the philosopher but ultimately can best be explored by psychoanalysts.[5] Because metaphor allows us to conceptualize familiar things in unfamiliar ways and unfamiliar things in familiar ways—he says that metaphors are intimately connected with all forms of learning and creativity in the arts, the exact sciences, and the human sciences, especially in personality development.

Indeed, an ever-larger volume of publications on these questions attests to the increasing fascination the issue of metaphor elicits today.

The Intersection of Poetry and Jungian Analysis through the Metaphor: In Creation You Are Created brings a vital benefit to psychoanalysts and psychotherapists of all theoretical orientations and will prove to be an indispensable reading for students of analytical psychology.

This book's core messages and key takeaways have the purpose

1. to demonstrate the vital intersection of poetry and the practice of Jungian analysis through the metaphor,
2. to contribute to an enriching language in the emotionally alive psychoanalytic process,
3. to validate that the mind functions metaphorically when faced with challenges requiring creativity,
4. to show that trauma leads to a degradation of metaphorical processes to mere repetition of compulsion,
5. to establish that interpretation uses the metaphorical process in the analysand as well as in the analyst to restore the diminished metaphor capacity and

6. to reveal that because metaphor delivers a deep sensorimotor experience to the person's physical and emotional system, both metaphors encountered in the analysis and in a good poem empower transformation.

NOTES

1. Ogden, T. H. "The Music of What Happens in Poetry and Psychoanalysis." *International Journal of Psychoanalysis* 80, 1999: 979–94.

2. Emilia Phillips. "Wislawa Szymborska's Influence on Poetry." *Ploughshares*, 2018.

3. Jung, C. G. *Collected Works* (Princeton, NJ: Princeton University Press, 1969), 82, 88–113, 129, 321, 323.

4. Hirshfield, Jane. "Poetry, Permeability, and Healing." Academy of American Poets, 2023, 1–2.

5. Borbely, A. "A Psychoanalytic Concept of Metaphor." *International Journal of Psychoanalysis* 79, 1998: 923–36.

Acknowledgments

I am grateful to Dr. Nadine Kaslow, who, when she was president of the American Psychological Association (APA), where we are both fellows, invited me to present my poems in an official meeting of the elected representatives at our annual convention. Dr. Kaslow, a psychology professor at Emory University, remains passionately involved in taking ballet classes and serving as a psychologist for the Atlanta Ballet. I am grateful to poets and writers for their support, inspiration, and loving presence across several countries, like the outstanding poets Carlos Drummond de Andrade and Joao Cabral de Melo Neto in Brazil, among many others. "Into the Blooming Night," for example, would not exist in English without the generous encouragement of Thomas Lux. He was the first to exhort me to write my poetry in his language. He was associated with my developing work at his discussion roundtables at the Georgia Institute of Technology in Atlanta, where I received my PhD in Neuroscience, at the Sarah Lawrence College Conference, Palm Beach Poetry Festivals, and Poetry @ Tech, among others. I express my deepest gratitude to Fred Fleischer as well.

Chapter 1

Metaphor

The Threshold of Consciousness

The American poet Mary Oliver (1935–2019), who won the National Book Award and the Pulitzer Prize, wrote:

> Instructions for living a life.
> Pay attention.[1]

The poet keeps her poem going by emphatically recommending being astonished by what we pay attention to and talking about it. To live life consciously consists of being alive in another dimension: the metaphorical life.

For that reason, Mary Oliver's instructions may guide not only poets but psychoanalysts.

Henry Seiden, in his book *The Motive for Metaphor: Brief Essays on Poetry and Psychoanalysis*, refers to that quest for consciousness through metaphor when he says: "Psychoanalysis deals in metaphor—in both our clinical exchanges and our theoretical formulations. We talk about one thing by referring to another."[2]

C. G. Jung himself uses a metaphor when he observes, in *Memories, Dreams, Reflections*: "As far as we can discern, the sole purpose of existence is to kindle a light in the darkness of mere being."[3]

In chapter 2, the author will present examples of metaphors from psychoanalysis. One could consider, for example, a situation that happened to her when she was a child as a student in Paris and an emotion she went through in São Paulo, Brazil. In addition, the author will share with the reader a poem that connects these two situations as a metaphor. These metaphors can clarify how our nervous system processes similar emotions in different modes and experiences different emotions with similar symbols. Through this process of metaphor (talking about one thing by referring to another), the analysand

and the analyst can better understand what is emotionally going on in the analytical session.

The use of metaphor goes back to the beginning of human thought. Relatively *recent* examples are found in poetry four thousand years old, in ancient Egyptian poetry, for example, in the epic of Gilgamesh. The prophetic dreams that both Gilgamesh and Enkidu describe in their story are used to show man's weaknesses in front of destiny. This is because, even as powerful as the two individuals are, they cannot change tragic events in their life paths. We can interpret Gilgamesh's dreams in that ancient text similarly to what we would do for the content of a contemporaneous client's dream. Notice that Ninsun, Gilgamesh's mother and also a goddess, interprets his dreams in which she appears. She is somewhat of a spiritual guide to Gilgamesh and Enkidu.

There is another type of metaphor we can talk about—visual metaphors. There is a serious opinion that the cave paintings of Lascaux, some 30,000 years old, are visual metaphors. A visual metaphor uses the pictorial representation of an object to suggest an association or similarity. Visual metaphors are visual tropes going back at least to Aristotle. They are highly structured images that stimulate viewers to understand one concept in terms of another. A visual metaphor creatively represents a concept, person, place, thing, or idea through an image that uses analogy or association.

Freud contends that our conscious behavior is only the visible 10 percent of our psyche—the tip of the iceberg, if you like. The mind is like an iceberg; it floats with one-seventh of its bulk above water. The deeper drivers of our behaviors—the other 90 percent—submerged in our subconscious or unconscious mind.

Indeed, *A Critical Dictionary of Jungian Analysis* refers to metaphor as "The definition and exploration of one thing by reference to the image of another. Metaphor is used as a conscious poetic device. Storytellers and writers have always employed it to suggest the subtleties of mystery or as an aid when trying to "express the inexpressible." Myth, ritual, and religion make use of metaphors.[4]

Jung's acknowledgment of a deep reservoir of irrepresentable images called archetypes in the psyche, his definition of the symbol as the best possible expression of an as-yet-undisclosed fact, his insistence that interpretation should remain faithful and as close as possible to the dream image, his likening of the psychic functioning of the Self to a God-image, and his affirmation that it is meaning rather than a treatment that relieves the suffering induced by a neurosis are all based on the supposition that the psyche reasons using images and that the closest rational equivalent is analogy or metaphor. Thus, his amplification method involves more than providing a more complete frame of reference for interpretation; it is a search for relevant metaphors. From the metaphor, the rational ego may ascertain or approximate an understanding of a psychic message. At the same time, the psyche can reorient itself by way of an enlarged image in consciousness.

This book's core messages and takeaways are:

1. to demonstrate the vital intersection of poetry and the practice of Jungian analysis through the metaphor,
2. to contribute to an enriching language in the emotionally alive psychoanalytic process,
3. to validate that the mind functions metaphorically when faced with challenges requiring creativity,
4. to show that trauma leads to a degradation of metaphorical processes to mere repetition of compulsion,
5. to observe that interpretation uses the metaphorical process in the analysand as well as in the analyst to restore the diminished metaphor capacity, and
6. to reveal that because metaphor delivers a deep sensorimotor experience to the person's physical and emotional system, both metaphors encountered in the analysis and in a good poem empower transformation.

The threshold of consciousness starts very early in humans. Implications of recent advances in neuroscience for an interpersonal neurobiological paradigm of psychology lead us to understand that the structure and function of the mind and brain are shaped by experiences, especially those involving affective processes. That's where the work of the right brain is fundamental.

In *Right Brain Psychotherapy*, for example, neuroscientist and psychoanalyst Allan Shore states that "The self-organization of the developing brain occurs in the context of a relationship with another brain, another self."[5]

From the very beginning of life, still in the uterus, the right hemisphere of the preverbal baby interacts—"converses," we could say—with the right hemisphere of the mother's brain. A similar process happens in psychoanalysis, between the analyst's and the analysand's brain.

Metaphor is crucial in that process. Working with dreams, emotions, and affective content, metaphor combines the opposites through the unconscious so these preverbal contents can be brought to the ego without the trauma of being dissociated.

NOTES

1. Oliver, Mary. *Devotions: The Selected Poems of Mary Oliver* (New York: Penguin Random House, 2017).

2. Seiden, Henry. *The Motive for Metaphor. Brief Essays on Poetry and Psychoanalysis* (New York: Routledge, 2018), 48.

3. Jung, C. G. *Collected Works* (Princeton, NJ: Princeton University Press, 1944), 130, 148, 400.

4. Samuels, Andrew, Bani Shorter, and Fred Plaut. *A Critical Dictionary of Jungian Analysis* (New York: Routledge, 1987), 72, 93.

5. Shore, Allan. *Right Brain Psychotherapy* (New York: W.W. Norton, 2019).

Chapter 2

In Creation, You Are Created

Carl Gustav Jung famously states in the book where his Zarathustra Seminars are collected that "In Creation, you are Created."[1] That affirmation is also the title Verena Kast has chosen for one of the seminars she teaches at the C.G. Jung Institut in Küsnacht, Switzerland, attended by students who are diploma candidates on their way to graduating as professional psychoanalysts.

In his *Zarathustra Seminars,* Jung affirms that the creative impulse is forever the maker of personality. Therefore, it is absolutely necessary that, in the process of individuation, everybody should become aware of his creative instinct, no matter how small it is.

He also says that "The human ego cannot live without creativity; it proves its existence by inventing something, by doing something on its own, out of the ordinary . . . And he alerts the reader that "I would not be able to give you any suitable definition of 'creative power' . . . we only know that it is, but how that is possible, we don't know."[2]

As the *Critical Dictionary of Jungian Analysis* says, a metaphor represents a powerful creative impulse.[3] It can be found sometimes in the language of everyday life and, more frequently, in powerful poetry and psychoanalytical practice. On the other hand, a specific choice of words in a metaphor can point to a particular comparison, expressing a precise reality. Still, an alternative analogy can represent the same situation or emotion using different words.

As an exercise in metaphor, the author proposes to think of the previous chapter—a prose narrative—and then presents a comparable situation as a poem. This will be an example of the personality of an individual working creatively with the specificities of their life.

Although she was born in Rio de Janeiro, Brazil, her family moved to Quito, Ecuador, when she was a few months old. Her father had been commissioned to supervise the geographic demarcation of a new boundary between Ecuador and Peru, as determined by the Rio de Janeiro treaty. Instead of learning Portuguese as her first language, the author learned Quechua and Spanish with those who worked in their house. These good people enjoyed teaching her about the world. Pointing to the sun, they would tell her its name is Inti. The mamacunas helped her learn how to walk. But also, she learned how to observe the llamas, listen to the flutes, and follow the movement of alert hands at the weave—and she was eager to follow the Inca intonations and warmth.

When she was four, her family returned from Ecuador to Brazil, where she learned Portuguese, and almost immediately, the family went to Paris, where the author was raised. As young children usually do, she learned the new language rapidly in that third country. But, as a new student at school, she noticed that she was not making close friends. That's when she discovered a social survival mode that came in handy: she could use her voice to sing to the other children. The vibration of their little chairs being brought around her at recess to listen to her singing stayed vivid in her memory. Some of these polite French kids would even say, "Mais c'est tout comme à la radio!" She was discovering the power of music. The author compares that situation—described in a prose narrative—to a poem.

The reader will find below "*Threshold of a Third Language,*" a poem she composed about a critical situation at her aunt's house in São Paulo just after her family came back from Quito and just before her family moved to Paris. In that poem, a similar metaphor as the one described to the reader as a new student at the school in France also happens.

You will find below "*Threshold of a Third Language,*" a poem the author composed about that critical situation. Would you say you can intuit a similar tone of emotion in the new student at the foreign school in Paris and in the metaphors describing the event at her aunt's house in São Paulo?

Would the reader say it is possible to intuit a similar tone of emotion in the new student at the foreign school in Paris and in the metaphors describing the event at her aunt's house in São Paulo?

Threshold of a Third Language

1.
The razor blade swift in his hand, father
was shaving. I dashed to climb the steps
carved into a hill behind my aunt's house,
to seek the fragrant signature of guava,
to say once more goodbye to Brazil,
the country I was born in but left—months old –
for another, where three snow-crowned volcanoes
like serene tigers slept not far from our porch.
In the Andes, four years went by, and my parents
assured me we would go back to a place
even better than Quito—so I wouldn't
have to clasp my arms around my dog,

my friends, both languages
the Inca mothers had taught me—to never
leave Ecuador, where the sky
turns up submerged in stars.
2.
Back in São Paulo, away
from the *mamacunas*, as I climbed
down from giving
a kiss of attention to the guava trees,
I saw flames. In a room behind the house, an iron
had turned clothes into a field of blazing tulips.
My aunt stood near the kitchen, talking to the parakeets,
although she did not speak the languages I spoke.
The iron is on fire! She smiled a "how-cute-you-are"
and kept chatting with the birds.
The iron. On fire! Quick!
She didn't move.
I pulled, but one by one,
she untangled my fingers from her skirt.
That's when I took off my sandal
and slapped her legs to push them forward.
Father appeared at the kitchen door,
razor in hand, his face hidden
behind a half mask of dragon foam.
3.
My flower-sandal vibrant in mid-air,
I turned to him: *The iron is burning!*
As his blade struck the tiles,
he yelled my words to my aunt, my words
she had refused to hear—although now
they sounded so different to me
I could not understand,
but she did and started screaming.
Neighbors rushed with pans,
ice buckets, hoses,
and streams of water raged against
tangerine flames licking, by now,
the other face of the house.
The parakeets stood still in awe.

The poem offers a musicality and a rhythm absent in the prose. For example, in the passage "That's when I took off one of my sandals/ and slapped her legs to push them forward," the reader can hear the sandal slapping the legs, helped by the sound of the initial syllables of <u>san</u>dal and <u>slap</u>ping. The rhythm is marked by the beats of the expression "to púsh thém fórward." In addition, the metaphors in the poem describe the situation of a child who appears as "a new student" in São Paulo—given that the language spoken there is a new one to her. At that moment, the musicality of the words shapes the dramatic meaning further:

> (my father) yelled my words to my aunt, my words
> she had refused to hear—although now
> they sounded so different to me
> I could not understand,
> but she did and started screaming.

The reader can hear, in the last verses of the stanza, how "she did" and "started screaming" sounds like a piercing scream, while "under*stánd*" and "st*árt*ed" burst into artillery salvos through their pounding "a."

One can also notice that the poem, with all its images—unfolds a series of metaphors. Like a dream, like an active imagination.

> *The iron is on fire!* She smiled "How cute you are"
> and kept chatting with the birds.
> *The iron. On fire! Quick!*
> She didn't move.
> I pulled, but one by one,
> she untangled my fingers from her skirt.
> That's when I took off my sandal
> and slapped her legs to push them forward.
> Father appeared at the kitchen door,
> razor in hand, his face hidden
> behind a half mask of dragon foam.

As one can see, the creativity and the "personality" brought together by that poem might manifest through large and small levels.

Indeed, the discernment of metaphors is a regular part of the practice of good therapists. The capacity to connect with the client's inner world depends on being open to the emotional, rhythmic, and sounding content of the metaphors they create and being capable of bringing them back to them in the therapist's interventions. That way, the client, who may feel like "a new student in a foreign school" in many ways, can feel that they are "heard" by the psychoanalyst and that their communication is valued. The psychoanalyst can also be more effective when alerting the client to an unconscious new development in their analysis if the therapist takes advantage of the creative images and the sounds the client spontaneously brings to the room.

When Jung alerts the reader that "I would not be able to give you any suitable definition of "creative power—we only know that it is, but how that is possible, we don't know," he is simply confirming what he has been saying all along in his work.[4] In any arts pursuit, in any creative exercise. It is impossible to know intellectually how, in creation, you are created precisely because creativity (as another metaphor) is a product of the conscious and the unconscious! It results from conscious and unconscious impulses—the intellectual desire to "explain" it cannot untangle the two processes.

Here's another example from the author's practice. One of her clients, who complained that it took him around two long hours to feel ready to start being active in the morning, told her that, this very day, he got up and immediately started doing what he had to do. "I was so surprised and delighted with this new turn," he exclaimed. "I am curious about why this happened," he added his body alert, sitting at the edge of the chair. "Why do you think this change has occurred?"

In his sixties, this client—one could call him John—had been mostly a thinking type and brought almost no dreams to his therapy. An engineer, he had been highly positioned in a large international bank and served in several countries. Because he had just been talking about dreams before he spoke about the morning surprise, the author observed: Well, a dream could be helpful here. He then exclaimed: I just had a dream last week! To which the analyst responded: Let's hear the dream.

The dream he brought was short and similar to his previous ones: he was at the bank, talking with some colleagues. The author did not feel that the image and associations he made brought a path to answer his question, but she clearly heard new, fresh energy in his voice.

"These colleagues were always contrarian to my good ideas of creating new solutions for the bank," he associated with his dream. "And, despite their negative opinions, I always had obtained outstanding results."

He then described three instances of success in detail where, in one of them, his implemented idea saved the bank 600 million dollars.

"You deserve warm congratulations, John,"—he author said in support of his decisive, successful action:

Although the large sum of money could be a symbol of "energy" and the therapist could try to work the metaphor from there—she started pondering to herself whether, in their work, there was something that could be felt "contrarian" to his good ideas. As she held for a moment, there was a pause. Then, out of the silence, his voice appeared to show even greater alertness.

"And then, of course, when I went to Buenos Aires, there was the kidnapping."

He had been her client for a while but had never mentioned any kidnapping.

"What kidnapping?" she asked.

He gestured toward an apparent distant time and explained:

"I was visiting Argentina as vice president of the international bank to implement a new platform there. At my arrival, at night, at Ezeiza International, the airport in Buenos Aires, one of the bank officers, Pepe, was waiting there for me."

"We met where the airplane arrived and went to gather my suitcase with documents and stuff from customs—he continued. As we were ready to leave the airport, three bandits—armed with machine guns—jumped in front of us and kidnapped us to a car that was waiting for them outside."

John was now very animated, and his body clearly remembered how the bandits handled them through the night outside the airport.

"They pushed us into the car, undressed us with nervous movements, and drove us around with our heads down, so we did not know where we were going. The bandits took all our belongings, including our clothes, shoes, and glasses. We were naked, at the bottom of the car, and the bandits drove us for what I believe was longer than one hour."

This was the Tupamaros' time, and that client knew the bandits were planning to ask a big ransom for them. He did not want them to learn that they were high officers of an international bank. He started trying to be friendly with one of the bandits and told that person that he had worked in Argentina before loved the country and was there now to visit his grandmother.

"And here's my cousin, Pepe," he said. These were the details he had invented at the moment.

"We finally arrived at a deserted field,"—John continued—his arms describing a large, empty space. The bandits led us out of the car and discussed what to do next. For some reason, they went somewhere else and told us to stay there. That was around 3:00 a.m., and the darkened field was deserted. I looked around and saw a well. I told Pepe to jump into the well and be as still and silent as possible. I also jumped into that well—which had no water and was around two meters deep. When the bandits returned, they did not find us and did not have the idea to investigate the well."

"We waited there for a long hour or more"—John told his analyst—"and, believing the bandits were gone, we managed to get out of the well. We did not know where we were, had no clothes or shoes, and I had to guide Pepe by the hand because he could not see without his glasses."

"We walked for a long time until we saw a highway where cars were going in one direction—but not one of them stopped for us, naked fellows, late at night. So, we kept going in the same direction as the cars until we arrived at the modest house of a laborer, who was very kind to provide us with some old clothes. There, Pepe called his brother, who came to rescue us."

The next day, as planned, the author's client was at the bank for the meeting and, that evening boarded the plane which would bring him to the country where he was going next.

For the analyst, all this dramatic story about kidnapping appeared to start connecting with John's question earlier in their session: where did the energy he had felt that morning—many years later—come from? What had changed?

After testing his associations, the psychoanalyst said: The unconscious speaks to us through symbols, through metaphors. What your unconscious is now telling us, with that powerful story that you associated with the initial dream, is that the opportunity to discover just-released energy in yourself is at hand.

I had thought—she offered—while I was listening to his story that hewas coming out of challenging times. He had to close his business in his country (due to the world financial crisis) and, for years, had tried to reinvent himself in a foreign country with some success.

"The new business you are creating now," the author said, "and the positive results obtained from it recently appeared to me as you are feeling as 'coming out of the well.' And with that, you feel now aware of a type of energy you have missed for a long time."

With that intervention, based on Jungian literature on healing trauma, the analyst was bringing *the well metaphor* to the client's attention—with the purpose of reconnecting the repressed energy in his inner world to his recent developments. She had in mind what Jung himself said in *Modern Man in Search of a Soul*: "We must follow nature as a guide. What the (therapist) then does is less a question of treatment than of developing the creative possibilities latent in the patient himself."[5]

That "coming out of the well" metaphor not only represented a financial matter. Still, it told them about the energy that had been "sequestered" in the unconscious and guarded by "bandits with machine guns," who took everything from John, even his clothes, shoes, and glasses. He felt like having to succeed "at night, with no orientation."

The author shared with her client that, as a protagonist of this vivid story he had just told her, he had accomplished just what needed to be accomplished in developing what she called his *individuation.* She suggested that the same incredible new energy he felt that morning, that stimulating emotion, could relate to his *coming out of the well* in his present life: a powerfully good prognostic. They continued their astonishing discovery and therapeutical work from there—reinvigorated by the metaphor John's unconscious had offered them in that session.

On the other hand, we could connect the situation experienced by John and Pepe that night—apparently lost from their points of reference—with the next chapter in this book, the Incas looking at the night sky on top of the Andes mountains. Like poets or other creators, the Incas could be trying to make sense of an unknown language—a discussion that could remind us of metaphors in poetry.

NOTES

1. Jung, C. G. *Collected Works* (Princeton NJ: Princeton University Press, 1944), 130, 148, 400.
2. Jung, C. G. *Nietzsche's Zarathustra: Notes of the Seminar Given in 1934–1939* (Princeton, NJ: Princeton University Press, 1989), 667, 745, 937.
3. Samuels, Andrew, Bani Shorter, and Fred Plaut. *A Critical Dictionary of Jungian Analysis,* (New York: Routledge, 1987), 72, 93.
4. Jung, C. G. *Collected Works* (Princeton, NJ: Princeton University Press, 1944), 130, 148, 400.
5. Jung, C. G. *Collected Works* (Princeton, NJ: Princeton University Press, 1944), 130, 148, 400.

Chapter 3

The Incas

Masters of Stars and Metaphors

Since time immemorial, even before the Babylonian astronomers, people worldwide looked at the sky at night. They discerned patterns formed by groups of stars, which we now call constellations. Greeks and Romans named many of them after their deities. Azteks had two of their calendars based on them. In Western cultures, we now have eighty-eight constellations, half of which were named by Ptolemy, a Greco-Roman astronomer who worked in the second century AD. All that time, around the world, folks used the stars to chart the seasons, navigate, and attribute divine significance to their lights in the sky.

The Incas, who established the Tauantinsuyo empire—which at its height stretched from Ecuador to Chile and had two capitals, Quito in Ecuador and Cuzco in Peru—went further. They grouped constellations into two different types: luminous and dark. In addition to the luminous ones—which the Incas determined were inanimate—they also focused on the darkness *between* the stars and named the shapes they discerned there, which they believed were alive. These dark cloud constellations were part of dark smudges in the Milky Way and represented the living forms of animals with which the Incas were familiar. They expressed them as *a metaphor*.

The author considers the dark and luminous constellations worshipped by the Incas as reminiscent of metaphors representing opposites in the personal and collective unconscious, as well as the images so crucial to Jung's research in archetypal theory. In the Inca astronomers' view, the luminous and the dark representations appear together and, in a sense, dialogue with each other.

In the Inca sky, Mayu—the Milky Way—is a life-giving river where the shadows of foxes, toads, partridges, and serpents come to drink. The larger and most influential constellation of darkness was the Yacana, the Llama, representing a mother llama and a baby llama (called a *cria*) drinking its mother's milk. Yacana is a dark-cloud constellation. Her eye, though, consists of two stars in the Centaurus constellation, Alpha Centauri and Beta Centauri. Here again, the dark and the luminous come together.

Yacana rises over Cuzco's sacred, ancient capital every November, and there, the llama and her child are worshipped during festivals. Llama and baby llama are believed to be the offspring of Inti, the sun god. That information is also interesting and makes sense if we look at it from the Jungian point of view: the sun giving birth to living darkness.

As we see, like John and his colleague, Pepe, whom we discussed in the previous chapter, advancing through the darkness of the night, the Incas labored to orientate themselves, make sense of the world, and, in so doing, created their dark and luminous metaphors. In fact, scientific discoveries have shown that Machu Picchu's structures were built to observe and worship the stars. From these structures, at 2.400 meters above sea level, in the Andes Mountains where the Incas lived, their astronomers tracked summer and winter solstices and the Moon's movement.

Even before there was appropriate accommodation for visitors, the author went to Macchu Picchu twice—a challenging place to get to—and was always stunned.

One of the narratives she remembers well was that there was an essential task among the Inca priests that they had to accomplish each year. They had to tie the sun god, Inti, at the solstice with their prayers and "alchemy" and bring it back the following year.

Considering this metaphor, we can understand that, in the Inca society, the essence of their livelihood depended on bringing the sun back from the shadows—a powerful metaphor in an analytic case as well. Which, in turn, went hand in hand with the power attributed to their priests. This, again, demonstrates the power of the metaphor.

Before arriving at that level of complexity, though, the Incas and other ancient people needed to develop a foundational utensil: language. Indeed, before we enter the specificities of metaphor in poetry and Jungian analytic practice, it should be noted that these metaphorical processes in language—in a professional analytical room and in a poem—are understood and generated by the same areas in the human brain. They are part of the same language that enables information sharing and our predictions about the world. Language allows us to produce poetry and a possible healing interpretation through which feelings can be expressed and speculate about things or events that may never become real. As Aristotle famously said: "It is a mark of an educated mind to be able to entertain a thought without accepting it." That observation brings us to another crucial foundational tool: imagination (more about this later).

Indeed, humans and animals communicate through multiple modalities, such as sight, odor, and touch. In a special issue of *Science Magazine*, the researchers focused on sound communication—particularly language. How does the brain produce and interpret language? Given the fundamental importance of communication in our society, it is no surprise that such a large part of the human brain is engaged in language processing. Syntax, grammar, and word selection define common ground and differentiate distinct human languages.[1]

Although language, and therefore spoken word or speech, is often considered unique to humans, the past several decades have seen a surge in nonhuman animal studies informing us about human spoken language. For instance, research about how birds learn their songs from their "tutors" (in the zebra finch, for example, in general, from the father) started modern studies on how human babies learn a language.

Human language allows us to create infinite ideas from a finite set of basic building blocks. What is the neurobiology of this combinatory system? Neuroscience has begun to dissect the neural basis of natural language syntax and semantics by analyzing the basics of meaning composition, such as two-word phrases. This work has revealed a composition system that involves rapid peaking activity in the left anterior temporal lobe and later engagement of the medial prefrontal cortex. Both brain regions show evidence of shared processing between comprehension and production and between spoken and signed language. Surprisingly, *both appear to compute meaning, not syntactic structure*. This finding allows us to reflect on the extreme importance of the symbolic capacity in human consciousness development and the extreme importance of archetypal theory in Jung's work.

With his theory of archetypes operating as components of the collective unconscious, Jung sought to define the basis of human psychology. Practically alone among the in-depth psychologists of the twentieth century, he rejected the tabula rasa theory of human psychological development.

Indeed, he wrote:

> [It is] a mistake to suppose that the psyche of the newborn child is a *tabula rasa* in the sense that there is absolutely nothing in it. Insofar as the child is born with a differentiated brain that is predetermined by heredity and therefore individualized, it meets sensory stimuli coming from outside not with *any aptitudes, but with specific ones.*[2]

The archetypes form the basis from which these specific aptitudes proceed.

There is no human experience, nor would experience be possible at all without the intervention of a subjective aptitude. A subjective innate psychic structure allows a person to have experiences with a priori categories, which have by nature a collective character; they are images of parents, wives, and children *in general* and are not individual predestinations. We must, therefore, think of these images as lacking solid content. We must, therefore, call them control unconscious. They only acquire solidity, influence, and eventual consciousness in encountering empirical facts, which touch the unconscious aptitude and bring them to life. In a sense, they are the deposits of all our ancestral experiences but not the experiences themselves.[3]

All these factors, essential to our near and remote ancestors, will also be essential to us, for they are embedded in the inherited organic system.[4]

Apart from Jung, nearly all other twentieth-century psychologists and psychoanalysts, as well as sociologists and anthropologists, focused on the myriad ways that individuals differed from one another and attempted to account for these differences in terms of the cultural and social influences they had been subjected to in the course of growing up. On the contrary, Jung affirmed that scientific psychology must start with what human beings had in common before the study of individual differences could proceed with any hope of reaching meaningful or valid conclusions.

Jung's position brought him into conflict with Sigmund Freud. Whereas Freud insisted that the unconscious mind was entirely personal and peculiar to the individual and made up of repressed wishes and traumatic memories, Jung maintained that an additional phylogenetic layer (the "collective unconscious") incorporated the entire psychic potential of humankind.

Support for these notions came from the studies Jung conducted with his colleagues at the Burghölzli Hospital in Zurich into the delusions and hallucinations of schizophrenic patients. These researchers and Jung demonstrated that these motifs and images also occurred in myths, religions, and fairy tales worldwide (Jung 1956).

Jung concluded that a dynamic substratum must exist common to all humanity, based on which each individual builds his or her own life experience, developing a unique array of psychological characteristics. In other words, the collective unconscious archetypes provided the basic themes of human life on which each individual worked out his or her own sets of variations.

In chapter 6 of this book, the author will present and discuss several fairy tales that surfaced at different times and regions of the world, demonstrating that reality.

The author will also refer to the importance of metaphor in fairy tales, meaning that the projection of human situations in fairy tales' characters and the situations they bring to the room present another important healing resource to the practice of Jungian psychoanalysis.

Because archetypes of the collective unconscious are vividly present in fairy tales, Jungian psychoanalysts richly use them in professional practice. Indeed, stories presented in fairy tales frequently function like a mirror to the client and can be used as excellent metaphors. That's the reason they are included in this book.

The archetype is thus Jung's basic concept. It is one of the most important ideas to emerge in the twentieth century, possessing far-reaching implications for both the social and the natural sciences.

NOTES

1. Clayton, David. "Learning Birdsong by Imitation: Transforming Sensory Information into Vocal Imitation Allows Young Finches to Sing." (*Science Magazine* 366, no. 6461, 2019), 33.
2. Jung, C. G. *Collected Works* (Princeton NJ: Princeton University Press, 1944), 130, 148, 400.
3. Ibid.
4. Ibid.

Chapter 4

The Powerful Image

The Metaphorical Mind

SYMBOLIC CAPACITY AND SYMBOL FORMATION

Symbolic capacity is a necessary ability needed for producing and understanding metaphors. That is the foundation of this chapter. For both dyads, the one formed by the psychoanalyst and the analysand and the one uniting the poet and the reader, the lover of poetry, symbolic capacity is crucial. To illustrate, here's a poem by the American poet Jane Hirshfield (1953).

In her poem "Autumn," Hirshfield starts by saying:

> Again, the wind
> flakes gold leaf from the trees.[1]

Then, she details what happens next: the painting darkens—as if a thousand penitents kissed an icon till it thinned back to the bare wood. The metaphors describe autumn scenery in the poem's original lines. In "Autumn," the reader can enjoy numerous observations about the images, the music of the wind brought to the reader by the sound of the letters *ss,* and the perception of that sound turned into an icon. Two high notes, though, are extremely important.[2]

First, using "flakes" as a verb empowers the image of the wind taking gold leaves from the trees. And the symbolic comparison (i.e., metaphor) that a thousand penitents kiss the icon thin till it turns to bare wood vigorously reproduces what the wind does to the trees. The "penitents" in the poem appear to consider the beauty of the poetic lines sacred.[3]

"Autumn" is a marvelous poem, and we can enjoy numerous observations about the images, the music of the wind brought to the reader by the sound of the letters *ss*, the rhythm, and the economy of its condensed form. Magic. And all this beauty and richness in only eight lines—which would not be possible without symbolic capacity—from the poet and from the reader.

Certainly, the poet is exercising her consciousness—and how her imagery appears symbolized in the poem. What would Jane Hirshfield's poem be without the symbolic dimension of language?

Other rich examples of symbolic capacity and symbol formation can be found in the work of the poet Hilda Doolittle, known as H.D. (1886–1961). *Helen in Egypt*, as extensively studied by Kristina Marie Darling in *Stylistic Innovation, Conscious Experience, and the Self in Modernist Women's Poetry*: *An Imagist Turned Philosopher.*

Truly, as a therapist, the author must be alert in her own symbolic capacity to allow the client's symbolization to be alive in the room. On the other hand, it is also important to probe whether a new client who presents for analysis can navigate and enter the harbor of metaphor's symbolic language. For example, in children, there are cases where the kid is so aligned with material objects and the strict, heavily enforced norms at home that free play with symbolization demands time and effort to surface in the analysis.

Mark Winborn, in *Working with Disruptions in Symbolic Capacity in Jungian Analysis: Theory and Practice,* a seminar he presented to the Moscow Association for Analytical Psychology Post-Graduate Studies Program in Moscow, Russia, states:

> Symbolization is at the very core of Analytical Psychology. Terms like myth, image, imaginal, symbol, and mythopoetic are all based on the notion of symbolization. Jung says the psyche is mythopoetic, meaning that the psyche creates myths, and myths are symbolic metaphors for ways of being, understanding, and experiencing. Symbols originate from an in-between place.[4]

That place between body and spirit can engage and integrate feeling, thought, and the soul.

Without the capacity to form symbols, there is little possibility of something coming alive. Symbols allow us to see, feel, and speak about a living connection between elements of experience and form the building blocks for transformation and the unfolding of the individuation process.[5]

In addition to agreeing with Winborn's quoted passage, the author clarifies what Jungian analysts call *individuation.* Jung says that the "Principium Individuationis" is the creature's essence. One of the earliest instances of the term "*individuation*" appearing in Jung's work occurs in a text from the year 1916 under the Latin title "Septem Sermones ad Mortuos" ("Seven Sermons to the Dead") to be found on page 7 of the Principle of Individuation.[6]

In becoming a person, we must create distinctions and separateness. The pleroma—in contrast to the individual (*creatura*) – contains all possible psychological facets but without distinction. It is the *psychic material*, the Great

Mother, from which everything that can become conscious will emerge. The fundamental principle of the *pleroma*, then, is inclusion without distinction.

On the other hand, the fundamental principle of individuation is essential to the human being—to distinguish oneself from one's surroundings. This is the drive the analyst refers to in Jungian analysis and stimulates their clients to progress toward becoming who they really are, as the analytical process takes place.

As Brigitte Egger says, based on Jung's theory, "the symbol can be experienced as a revelation and used as a translation key. If becoming possessed by a symbol imprisons us, entering into dialog with it liberates energy."[7]

As we focus on Jung's concepts of *symbol* and *archetype*—and convey examples of the interface of symbolic metaphors in client's cases and poetry—we might be reminded of Pech-Merle.

That French cave discovered by two teenagers in 1922 is a place where prehistoric artists stretched out their hands toward the wall and blew red ochre and black cinder over them, leaving their signature visible to us 20,000 years later. These hands and the astounding animal paintings surrounding them attest to the persistent human effort toward consciousness and the timeless social dedication to symbolic images.

Indeed, the oldest cave art points to Neanderthal symbolic behavior. In Spain's La Paciega Cave, Neanderthals' lines were embellished by later artists. According to a team of dating experts and archaeologists, recently cited by *Science Magazine,* simple creations from three caves in that area all date to more than 64,800 years ago, at least 20,000 years before modern humans reached Europe. Shells from a fourth Spanish cave, pigment-stained and pierced as if for use as body ornaments, are even older. These findings confirm, as well, the persistent human effort toward symbolization.[8]

METAPHOR AS A CONTAINER OF OPPOSITES: ENCOMPASSING BOTH

In *Psychology and Alchemy*, Jung affirms, "The symbol is neither abstract nor concrete, neither rational nor irrational, neither real nor unreal. It is always both." And, in *The Transcendent Function*, he states that the symbol is "the best possible expression of a complex fact not yet clearly apprehended by consciousness."[9]

Edward Edinger, the distinguished Jungian analyst, talking about Greek mythology and poetry, says—in his book *The Eternal Drama. The Inner Meaning of Greek Mythology*: "Of course, poets know all about this spiritual nourishment because they are all mythologists."[10]

In fact, as the reader can see in *Autumn*, Jane Hirshfield's poem, she makes mythical images visible.

Edinger amplifies his idea that poets are mythologists when he says:

> They live in constant awareness of the archetypal powers. Theodore Dreiser, a literary man who had something of a poet in him, gave an impeccable description of the reality of a mythical image when he said that he knew that the Furies existed because he had heard the beating of their wings.[11]

In this passage, Edinger calls our attention to the fact that Dreiser appears to interact with the Furies like he inhabits their mythical space. That's because the metaphor—a container of opposites encompassing both—is simultaneously an inner and an outer experience.

In her comparative study *From Freud to Jung*, Liliane Frey-Rohn suggests that "one of Jung's most remarkable insights was the concept of the symbol as a mediator, unifying the opposites of conscious and unconscious."[12]

She points out that the symbol is an *image* that manifests the primordial psychic background not yet rationally shaped but which, conversely, participates in conscious reality.[13]

Frey-Rohn's analysis demonstrates that every psychic product, including the metaphor if it is the best possible expression, may be regarded as a symbol as yet unknown or only relatively known. For that reason, a dream, a poem, and a fairy tale, functioning as a metaphor, is a symbol that may serve as a vessel containing other symbols in its journey to us.

From its etymology, the word *symbol* started to designate the union of two opposites: something conscious—known—with something unconscious—unknown. Because what is unknown has an affective value, the symbol always brings about emotion to the perceiver. Here's the numinous aspect of the symbol: it points to a connection between the conscious and the unconscious dimensions of the same phenomenon. Even when we rationally know the design and colors of a flag, it is difficult not to feel emotion when we see it waving at a significant international event. Thus, the symbol represents the connection with the energy needed to produce events that alter things. They surface from the archetypal depths of the personality—the collective unconscious—and build a bridge between the conscious and the unconscious.

We could be reminded of the Incas looking at their starry sky, being astonished, and starting to work with metaphors—using images—as they created constellations.

Mircea Eliade, a renowned Romanian researcher in the area of the psychology of religion, mythology, and magic, argues in his study *Images and Symbols* that:

> The ethnologist of today has not only grasped the importance of symbolism in archaic thinking but has seen its intrinsic coherence, its validity, its speculative audacity, its "nobility." . . . The greatest merit of C. G Jung is that he has gone further than Freudian psychoanalysis on the plane of psychology itself and has thus restored the spiritual significance of the image.[14]

That's what Eliade means by the word "nobility"—the spiritual significance of the image that Freud, given his theoretical distance from spiritual matters, would not decodify.

Symbols contain elements of spirit and instinct, image, and drive—and are the great organizers of libido. The reason that symbols have such importance for Jung derives from their ability to *transform natural energy into cultural and spiritual forms.* In his essay *On Psychic Energy*, Jung provides a formal theoretical account of transformations and how these changes occur. Indeed, a fundamental distinction between Jung's and Freud's theories—*and the reason for the end of their collaboration*—resides in the difference between *transformation* and *sublimation.*[15]

Freud believed that humans could sublimate libidinal desires, but that resulting sublimation would substitute for those desired real objects. From that point of view, the libido would always wish to return to the respective mother, father, and childhood, to Oedipal fantasies. Freudian analysis, thus, would be continuously reductive.

In contrast, Jung posits that, whereas the infant's libido initially seeks the mother's body due to its necessity for survival, later on, the impulse will flow through other gradients—into procreation, in adulthood, for example. When the libido encounters an image analogue, a spiritual metaphor, though, it will go in that direction, not because this is a substitute for sexual desire, but because it is its fundamental goal to do so. For Jung, this is a transformation of libido. Culture is created from such transformations—like in the case of a gorgeous poem, the music composed for an oboe, a delicious dinner at an excellent restaurant, or the work that organizations like Médicins Sans Frontières accomplish.

The following quote from Jung demonstrates that assertion:

> Every advance in culture is, psychologically, an extension of consciousness, a coming to consciousness that can only occur through the perception of distinction. Therefore, an advance always begins with individuation, that is to say, with the individual, conscious of his isolation, cutting a new path through the hitherto untrodden territory.[16]

To do this, the person must first return to the fundamental facts of his or her own being, irrespective of the authority and tradition of the culture to which he or she belongs. The person must allow himself or herself to become conscious of his distinctiveness. "Reflection" should be understood not simply as an act of thought but rather as an attitude. It is a privilege born of human freedom in contradistinction to the compulsion of natural law.

That important distinction between Jungian and Freudian theories leads us to understand better the act of becoming conscious. In the same text, Jung concludes:

> As the word itself testifies ("reflection" means literally "bending back"), reflection is a spiritual act that runs counter to the natural process; an act whereby we stop, call something to mind, form a picture, and take up a relation to and come to terms with what we have seen. It should, therefore, be understood as an act of becoming conscious.[17]

As we can see, Jung believes that human nature leads to culture formation, the creation of symbols, and the containment of energy so that its flow can be directed toward these spiritual and mental contents. The tension between the archetype and instinct in the symbol makes the symbol alive—the same way it makes the metaphor alive. Our minds are metaphorical.

Indeed, a powerful image frequently appears as an essential element energizing both metaphors we admire in poetry and metaphors generated in the dialog between client and analyst.

Although Jung intermingled the words "symbol" and "image" at different times in his professional career, using these words almost as synonyms for one another, in the long run, he conceived of the image as both prior to and greater than the sum of its symbolic components. He affirms: "The image is a condensed expression of the psychic situation as a whole, and not merely, or even predominantly, of unconscious contents pure and simple."[18]

The implication is that—as *The Critical Dictionary of Jungian Analysis* states—whereas Jung's understanding of the image might have changed in the course of his lifetime, "his most telling discovery, verified empirically, could be that the psyche itself does not proceed 'scientifically,' that is, by way of hypothesis and model, but *imagistically,* that is, through myth and metaphor."[19]

The dictionary clarifies: "Because the image is a *container* of opposites, in contradistinction to the symbol, which is *a mediator* of opposites, it does not adhere to any one position, but elements of it can be found in either. For example, the image of the anima is both an inner and an outer experience at the same time."[20]

Verena Kast, in a personal communication with the author, summed up that critical discernment as follows: "The generic term is a *picture*, or it is about processes in pictures—especially in poems. The pictures can be used metaphorically, or they can be understood as symbols."[21]

For example, we can revisit "Autumn," Jane Hirshfield's poem, and connect this discussion of pictures and distinctiveness back to poetry.

We can see, then, how the use of a powerful image—meaning the use of metaphor—and the capacity for individuation are crucial in poetry and analysis.

Indeed, Kast's evaluation reminds us of the clinical richness of active imagination, where images of a dream (or a poem) are brought to dialogue with the conscious ego and the dreamer's (or reader's) emotions.

METAPHOR REFERRING TO ARCHETYPE

The contemporary view of metaphor is grounded in its generalization from rhetoric to cognitive process. In that way, David Leary proposed that metaphor is not only "a distinctive use of language" but "more fundamentally a form of *thought*, having basic epistemological functions."

James Hillman supported that view when he wrote: "Metaphors are more than ways of speaking; they are ways of perceiving, feeling, and existing."[22]

Hillman attempted to clarify the concept of *image* in his book *Re-Visioning Psychology*. He says in his introduction:

> Freud and Jung are psychological masters, not that we may follow them in becoming Freudian and Jungian, but that we may follow them in becoming psychological. Here, psychology is conceived as a necessary activity of the psyche that constructs vessels and breaks them to deepen and intensify the experience.[23]

In fact, Hillman's research shows that, in Jungian psychology, one of the therapist's functions is to enable the client to progress in the reencountering and reexperiencing of themselves.

Referring to archetypes, metaphor implies a very specific way of looking at them. Archetypes are challenging to explain because they tend to be metaphors rather than things. The problem with literally describing an archetype is our tendency to express them as images. We tend to say what "they are like"—we enter into an imaginative discourse style. Jung—who reintroduced the ancient idea of archetype into modern psychology—tells us to imagine archetypes as *the deepest psychic functioning patterns, the roots* of the soul governing our perspectives of ourselves and the world. When we talk about "matter," "God," "energy," "life," "health," "society," and "art," we are referring to fundamental metaphors—possibly archetypes in themselves, containing whole worlds together, which cannot be effectively circumscribed or pointed to. Speaking of archetypes, we are using translations from one metaphor to another.

Marc Slavin, in his book *Metaphor and Imaginal Psychology. A Hermetic Reflection* explores the significance of metaphor in post-Jungian psychology. He says about Images: "Hillman drew the imaginal idea of psychology from two sources: Jung, who said that 'image *is* psyche,' and Henry Corbin, for whom the *mundus imaginalis* constituted an interzone between spirit and matter."[24]

Hillman hoped to discern a perspective that could be called the soul's own by emphasizing image. Imaginal psychology sees the psyche not as an object but as a creative process. The unconscious becomes an animating principle, "the imaginal power of the psyche."

This de-objectivation attempts to revert from the "egoization of the psyche" to an articulation of the psyche's own logic, seen as *poietic* and agonistic. The reformulation of the psyche-logos as aesthetics frees the unconscious from its analytic metaphorization in which it is understood from the perspective of the ego's persistent urge to solve problems, cure illness, and bring all matters into productive alignment.

This passage about articulating the psyche's own logic, seen as both creative and polemic, supports this chapters's premise. Considering Jung's assertion that "image *is* psyche" and that both the poet and the analyst deal with the image (or metaphor) all the time, we can see that the exercise of *poiesis* is deeply connected to both of them. Indeed, *poiesis*—etymologically derived from an ancient Greek term that means "to make," and which is also experienced in the word *poetry*—represents that activity in which a person brings something into being that did not exist previously.

Reflecting on this chapter's title—In Creation, You Are Created—let us recall that Jung used the term *archetypal image* to refer to creativity. He affirms that the creative process consists of the unconscious activation of an archetypal image and elaborating and shaping this image into the finished work. By giving it shape, the artist translates it into the language of the present, making it possible for us to find our way back to the deepest springs of life.[25]

ASTONISHMENT AND IMAGINATION

One needs to exercise imagination and astonishment to successfully create a useful metaphor. Or the other way around.

Wisława Szymborska (1923–2012), the Polish poet who won the Nobel Prize in 1996, said in her acceptance lecture, "The Poet and the World": "Poets, if they are genuine, must keep repeating, 'I don't know.'"[26]

The phrase "I don't know" is small, Szymborska says, but it flies on mighty wings. It expands our lives to include the spaces within us and these outer expanses in which our tiny Earth hangs suspended. It is the core of curiosity, and paradoxically, it's perhaps the phrase most integral to empathy.[27]

In the opinion of several critics, Szymborska's poetry demonstrates this ideal through its allegiance to astonishment, a feature that stands as her most lasting influence in poetry. Astonishment is a surrender born out of inquisitive and active humility; its sympathetic refrain of "I don't know" offers poetry space for a wandering imagination.

The phrase "I don't know" is small, Wislawa says, but it flies on mighty wings. It expands our lives to include the spaces within us and these outer expanses in which our tiny Earth hangs suspended. It is the core of curiosity, and paradoxically, it's perhaps the phrase most integral to empathy.[28]

Empathy, of course, is important for poetry. Writing or reading a poem is an act of empathy because it honors and dialogues with *the other.*

I don't know doesn't mean *I don't want to know,* says *Wyslawa,* but rather *I want to know more*. It is an allowance of space meant to be filled. It makes room for the other and for other people.[29]

In fact, Szymborska contends that

> Poems are not parades of the known but rather failed attempts at knowing—much like the essay, named thus for the Old French word meaning "to try," *essayer*. And yet, poems are equally amazed by what they are, and what they are not, what they can contain, and what they cannot.[30]

Szymborska's poem "Among the Multitudes" features a speaker astonished at what she is and what she isn't.[31] She could have been

> Someone much less fortunate
> bred for my fur or Christmas dinner.[32]

Imagining what might have been serving Szymborska as a tool to craft drama in her poetry, this poem, however, emphasizes astonishment to make clear that it is an integral part of her identity. The poet concludes:

> I might have been myself minus amazement,
> that is someone completely different.[33]

At first, it seems that amazement is only a part of the speaker's self, but the last line changes that perception. Without her amazement, she is "someone completely different." We might connect the astonishment Szymborska is referring to as an integral part of her individuated self to the metaphor in Mary Oliver's poem, where she invites the reader to be astonished.

Astonishment is also necessary for the use of irony, which we find plenty of in Szymborska's work. The Nobel Prize in Literature 1996 was awarded to her "for poetry that with ironic precision allows the historical and biological context to come to light in fragments of human reality."[34]

On the other hand, as Szymborska considers geologic time and distant planets, her inner life and memory are among the most astonishing subjects for the poet. Let us consider, for instance, her poem "Memory Finally," from *No End of Fun.*

> Memory finally found what it was after
> My mother has turned up, my father has been spotted.[35]

The poem informs the reader that she saw a table and two chairs (like in a dream). Mother and father sat. They were hers again, alive again for her, she says.

When we read these lines of metaphors by Szymborska—with both seeing the scene and feeling the emotion—we can immediately think of active imagination. As the reader might know, active imagination is a therapy method that, by concentrating the client's attention on an image—from dreams or otherwise—aims to facilitate the start of an inner dialogue between the conscious and the unconscious of that person. One might say that's the same road through which successful metaphors—in poetry and therapy—bring unknown contents hiding behind the bushes to a more efficient light.

In her book *Imagination as Space of Freedom,* Verena Kast points out that "It is essential to truly experience emotions because this both frees energies for action and enables one to experience one's relationship with oneself."[36]

We can compare that space of freedom to the work of poetry. Kast adds:

> Psychotherapeutic work with and out of images has its antecedents in work with dream images in Freud, Jung, and others. Dealing with our dream images and all other images, we come to see that they tell us something about ourselves and that they can also bring about changes in our experiences of ourselves and the world.[37]

Through compelling images, intuition, musicality, and rhythm, good poetry brings about changes in the experiences of oneself and the world—to the poet and the lover of poetry, who can allow inner space for the poem to expand. Indeed, when Wisława Szymborska contends that "Poetry is the operative exercise of not knowing," and when she tells us that without her astonishment, she would have been "someone completely different," we might be reminded of Jung considering his initial attempt to interpret a dream and amazingly saying: "I have no idea what this dream is about."[38] As we discuss great poets and gifted analysts, we can see that both work deeply in the unconscious, with astonishment, imagination, and metaphor.

In closing this chapter, one could mention a poem "Sleepers" by the American poet Arthur Sze (1950). The author could say that this work's metaphors point to imagination and astonishment. Arthur Sze shares with the reader the way the poem came into existence. He says:

> One morning, I saw a black-chinned hummingbird land on a metal wire and stay there for a long time. In that interval, the speaker of the poem moves from northern New Mexico to Venice, Italy, then back to New Mexico. Sze tells the reader that he does not know how the poem wrote itself, but he trusted the spell.[39]

The poet starts setting the scene, establishing expectations for a potential reader. The narrative is described between the arrival of the hummingbird and its departure. Repetitions come within a metronome: "five seconds," at first light, before first light, a mechanic untwists a plug.[40]

> Apparently, the poet wants to be precise, in contrast to the poem's
> title: Sleepers
> A black-chinned hummingbird lands
> on a metal wire and rests for five seconds.[41]

Then, the poet proceeds to a sequence of five-second episodes: a pianist lowers his head and rests his hands on the keys for five seconds. Reproducing the hummingbird, which rests for five seconds on the metal wire, the pianist lowers his head and rests his hand on the keys—which generally happens at the end of a musical occurrence, not at the start.

NOTES

1. Hirshfield, Jane. "Autumn." *The Paris Review* 109.
2. Ibid.
3. Ibid.
4. Winborn, M. "Interpretation in Jungian Analysis." *Art and Technique*, 2019, 21.
5. Ibid.
6. Ibid.
7. Egger, Brigitte. *The Symbol in Analytical Psychology: A Vivifying Experience,* 2017.
8. "Oldest Dated Cave Art Points to Neandertal Symbolic Behavior." *Science Magazine* 359, no. 6378, 2018), 852 and 912.

9. Jung, C. G. *Collected Works* (Princeton NJ: Princeton University Press, 1944), 130, 148, 400.

10. Edinger, E. *The Eternal Drama: The Inner Meaning of Greek Mythology* (Boston: Shambhala Publications, Inc., 1994), 83.

11. Ibid.

12. Frey-Rohn, L. *From Freud to Jung. Comparative Study of the Psychology of the Unconscious* (Boston. Shambhala Publications, Inc., 1990), 265.

13. Ibid.

14. Ibid.

15. Ibid.

16. Jung, C. G. *Collected Works* (Princeton NJ: Princeton University Press, 1944), 130, 148, 400.

17. Ibid.

18. Ibid.

19. Samuels, Andrew, Bani Shorter and Fred Plaut. *A Critical Dictionary of Jungian Analysis,* (New York: Routledge, 1987), 72, 93.

20. Ibid.

21. Kast, V. *Joy, Inspiration, and Hope* (College Station: Texas A&M University Press, 1991), 4.

22. Hillman, J. *Re-Visioning Psychology* (New York: Harper & Row, 1975), 156.

23. Ibid.

24. Slavin, Marc. *Metaphor and Imaginal Psychology. A Hermetic Reflection* (New York: Routledge, 2018), 141.

25. Jung, C. G. *Collected Works* (Princeton, NJ: Princeton University Press, 1969), 82, 88–113, 129, 321, 323.

26. Emilia Phillips. "Wislawa Szymborska's Influence on Poetry." (*Ploughshares*, 2018).

27. Ibid.

28. Ibid.

29. Ibid.

30. Ibid.

31. Ibid.

32. Ibid.

33. Ibid.

34. Ibid.

35. Ibid.

36. Kast, Verena. *Imagination as Space of Freedom. Dialogue Between the Ego and the Unconscious* (New York: International Publishing Corporation, 1993), 15.

37. Ibid.

38. Jung, C. G. *Collected Works* (Princeton, NJ: Princeton University Press, 1969), 82, 88–113, 129, 321, 323.

39. Sze, Arthur. "Sleepers." Academy of American Poets, 2019.

40. Ibid.

41. Ibid.

Chapter 5

Poetry as a Healing Resource

In his essay *On the Relation of Analytical Psychology to Poetry*, Jung refers to the poet's work as follows:

> Whoever speaks in primordial images speaks with a thousand voices; [the poet] enthralls and overpowers, while simultaneously, he lifts the idea he seeks to express out of the occasional and the transitory into the realm of the ever-enduring. He transmutes our personal destiny into the destiny of mankind and evokes in us all those beneficent forces that ever and anon have enabled humanity to find a refuge from every peril and to outlive the longest night.[1]

As one considers the writing and sharing of poetry as an essential act of testimony on our own and the world's individuation, one can also find shelter in poetry as a healing resource.

If the reader revisits "Autumn," the poem by Jane Hirshfield—which is presented in chapter 4—the reader will notice how it bridges the gap between the conscious and the unconscious and how the poet "speaks in a thousand voices," describing the penitents who traverse Autumn's darkness of this world and kiss the poem's icon till it thinned back to the bare wood" without diminishment.[2]

Still considering that poem, we can associate its content with what Jung affirms in *Poetry and Collective Unconscious*:

> [Poets] are always the first to divine the darkly moving mysterious currents and to express them, as best they can, in symbols that speak to us. They make known, like true prophets, the stirrings of the collective unconscious or, in the language of the Old Testament, or "the will of God," which in the course of time must inevitably come to the surface as a collective phenomenon.[3]

Later, in the same paper, Jung concludes: "We cannot, therefore, afford to be indifferent to the poets, since in their principal works and deepest inspirations they create from the very depths of the collective unconscious—could say 'the painting'—voicing aloud what others only dream."[4]

Robert Bly (1926–2021), an American contemporary poet, in his book *Leaping Poetry*, refers to that perception with a postmodern metaphor: "A poet who is 'leaping' jumps from an object soaked in unconscious substance to an object or idea soaked in conscious psychic substance."[5] The poet does this, says Bly, "with some arc of association which corresponds to the inner life of the objects; so that anyone sensitive to the inner life of objects can ride with him."[6] The implication of this observation—also applicable in the psychoanalytical relationship—points to the singular importance of the artistic leap that bridges the gap between conscious and unconscious thought in any great work of art, the process that he calls "riding on dragons."[7]

The same metaphor can be applied to the poem presented in chapter 4, "Sleepers," by Arthur Sze. In that poem, the poet is "leaping." If we read a few stanzas, we are immediately alert to that concept—although the poem "leaps" in its entirety, including ostinato notes and physical embrace.[8]

This is what we call, in poetry, "a list poem." It consists of a list of metaphors of conscious and unconscious experiences, that, in the end, form the poem's body, leap by leap.

In the next chapter of this book, the work of a few modern psychoanalysts based on novel neuroscience findings and their own intuition for the intensity of poetry will be considered. In the author's opinion, their research amplifies Jung's traditional view. These researchers aim not only at poetry's intellectual level but also at its compositional vibrancy, compelling music, rhythm, energy, and sensorimotor embodiment. They address what poetry has been for millennia, resounding with the transformative power it can carry.

One of these contemporary analysts we will study in the next chapter, Jeanine Marie Vivona, suggests: "This is an important area to explore. The words the poet elevates to art are at work in psychoanalysis all the time as a source of therapeutic action."[9] One could add to Vivona's words the reflection that the metaphor that works in analysis instigates therapeutic action *for the same reason* that a metaphor encountered in a poem delivers a deep sensorimotor experience to the reader's physical and emotional system. Poetry can contribute to healing for that exact same reason. Good poetry goes deep, and due to its embodiment, it provides a sensorimotor experience that brings about therapeutic power. This observation is based on what therapists have witnessed repeatedly: being embodied or grounded in sensorimotor experience is essential to healing.

INSIGHT

When we gain *insight*, we have a feeling, emotion, or thought that helps us know something essential about a person or thing. The word *in-sight*—formed by the prefix *in*—plus the English word *sight*—literally expresses *seeing inward*. From that perspective, the psychoanalyst Jeanine M. Vivona says:

> The experience of hearing a good poem or a good interpretation is of being understood and, at the same time, seeing something new about oneself that has been articulated by someone else from within that person's own experience. The change that can happen in hearing such language we call *insight*. Insight is not only knowledge, not only content. It is an experience of resonance with another person's vision of things.[10]

One can associate that hunger for insight and meaning with what the American Pulitzer Prize–winning poet William Carlos Williams (1883–1963) refers to in his poem "Asphodel, That Greeny Flower":

> Williams agrees that it is difficult to get the news from poems. He
> affirms, though, that
> Men die miserably every day
> for lack of what is found there.[11]

In search of that vividness, poetry scholars from Keele University opened up a "Poetry Pharmacy" in a Victorian shop in a small town in England in October 2019. There, visitors can participate in poetry classes, special day retreats, consultations, and prescriptions for poetry, which all focus on providing mental health support for the local community and emphasize the therapeutic benefits of poetry: We believe that poetry can do so much to match or alter a mood, to assist in so many ways with good mental health, says Deborah Alma, the pharmacy's designated "Emergency Poet."

Indeed, there are now, across the world, several groups engaged in what is known as poetry therapy. The author of this book has no personal experience with how they work. Still, there is, for instance, a National Association for Poetry Therapy in the United States, a nonprofit, interdisciplinary organization that—as they say on the Internet—supports and enhances the profession of poetry therapy. Its mission is to promote growth and healing through written and spoken language, symbolic expression, and story.

Considering insight, it would be useful to recall the psychoanalyst James Hillman because he sees what he calls the *soul* at work in imagination, dreams, fantasy, myth, and metaphor. He also sees the *soul* revealed in psychopathology, in the symptoms of psychological disorders. He wrote, in *Re-Visioning Psychology:*

> Therapy is a heavy word, bringing to mind the suffering of illness and what we go through to cure it. Therapy or analysis is not only something that analysis does to patients; it is a process that goes on intermittently in our individual soul-searching, our attempts at understanding our complexities, the critical attacks, prescriptions, and encouragements that we give ourselves. We are all in therapy all the time insofar as we are involved with soul-making.[12]

To illustrate the insight that poetic metaphors can bring to the reader, here is a quote from the American poet Ellen Bass (1947) in an interview for *Rattle.* She says:

> It is intimate to read or to write a poem, and when a poem is read—even across the centuries, across the continents—the poet and the reader have met. And metaphor is part of that.
>
> Originally, poets were priests, she continues. The word mattered. Even today, in Judaism, when the person reading the Torah portion reads aloud, someone stands next to the reader looking at the text, so if he makes an error, they correct it because it can't go into the air with a mistake because the sound of the words changes the world.[13]

Like in a dream, which presents itself as a metaphor, the image in a dialogue between a client and the analyst can be a tool for transformation. When the analyst focuses on an analogy with a patient, the clinician is, in a way, teaching his or her brain—and probably his or her sensorimotor state—to switch to a different mode. Indeed, the brain naturally does this. By using metaphor, we are activating a capacity innate in most humans. This change is what Edward Edinger refers to as using metaphor to facilitate therapeutic transformation—as a *coniunctio,* he says, a coming together of opposites.

To put his words in perspective, let us revisit a film together.

In *Il Postino* (the postman), the reader can specifically enjoy the dialogue between the Chilean poet Pablo Neruda (1904–1973) (International Peace Prize, 1950; Lenin Peace Prize, 1953; and the Nobel Prize in Literature, 1971) who was living in exile in Southern Italy and Mario, the Italian youth who brings him his mail. In the film scene, which the author would like to connect with metaphor in this chapter, we find Pablo and Mario sitting together, looking out over the ocean, and the poet creates a powerful, splendid image of the waves. Then, Neruda asks Mario what he thinks of his description of the sea.

> Mario: It's weird; it's weird how I felt while you were saying it.
>
> Neruda: How was that?
>
> Mario: I don't know. The words went back and forth.
>
> Neruda: Like the sea, then?

Mario: Exactly. Like the sea.

Neruda: That's the rhythm.

Mario: I felt seasick! Because—I can't explain it—I felt like a boat tossing around on those words.

Neruda: Like a boat tossing around on my words?

Mario: Yes!

Neruda: Do you know what you've done, Mario?

Mario: No, what?

Neruda: You've created a metaphor.

Mario: No!

Neruda: Yes, you really have.

Mario: But this doesn't count because I didn't mean to!

Neruda: You didn't have to. Images arise by themselves.

In that decisive moment, Mario discovered how to use his images as metaphors. He was learning to experience astonishment for the world's marvels and express the indescribable.

In his book *The Eternal Drama*, Edward Edinger emphasizes that astonishment when he says: "Poets know all about this spiritual nourishment because they are all mythologists, as we quoted him earlier. Poets make mythical images visible. They live in constant awareness of the archetypal powers, which are the inherited part of the Psyche, a hypothetical entity irrepresentable in itself and evident only through its manifestations."[14]

The author of this book could add that another powerful metaphor comes to mind in Greek mythology. In search of Medusa, Perseus finally sees her by way of his mirror shield and cuts off her head. Out of the severed head flies Pegasus, the winged horse, *the symbol of poetry.*

Reflecting on the "birth" of Pegasus, Edinger observes: "Here is a striking image of released libido. It is as if the decapitation of the Medusan horror had the effect of transforming the negative energy contained in her and releasing it into positive, creative power signified by the horse, a symbol of physical energy that is at the same time winged."[15]

We could undoubtedly associate Edinger's words with poetry in its capacity for transforming negative energy and releasing it into positive, creative power—in its capacity as a healing resource.

THE POET IS IN: MUSIC, RHYTHM, EMBODIMENT

Miles Davis, the famous American jazz trumpeter, bandleader, and composer (1926–1991) who helped define the course of jazz, said: "It takes a long time to learn how to play like yourself."

The author is delighted to translate Miles Davis's insight from the musical to the psychological realm: It takes a long time to find one's own path to individuation. And that's the same for a poet.

For instance, it took a long time for the Chilean poet Neruda to learn how to describe the ocean in such a rhythmic and compelling way that Mario felt that "the words went back and forth," and he was *like* "a boat tossing around on Neruda's words." That's exhilarating and beautiful.

As Ellen Bass says: Poetry is magic. And it is magic, partly because of the percussion of its rhythm and the captivating sound of its music, which brings a sensorimotor experience to the poet and the reader. We can *hear* the metrical "feet" in a line of poetry and understand how the ocean can become alive as sound. Here are a few examples of traditional poetry:

An *iamb* is a metrical foot consisting of one short (or unstressed) syllable followed by one long (or stressed) syllable. So, an *iambic* verse has one syllable not accentuated, followed by one accentuated. It sounds like this: "To strívе, to séek, to fínd, and nót, to yíeld."

An *anapest* is a metrical foot consisting of one short (or unstressed) syllable followed by one long (or stressed) syllable. It sounds this way: "And the shéen / of their spéars / was like stárs / on the séa."

A *dactyl* is a metrical foot consisting of one stressed syllable followed by two unstressed syllables or (in Greek and Latin) one long syllable followed by two short syllables. In accentual verse, often used in English, it is a stressed syllable followed by two unstressed syllables—the opposite is the *anapest*, with two unaccented syllables followed by one accented syllable.

It sounds like this: "Táke ~her ~up / tén~der~ly."

As an exercise, the author would suggest that one could read aloud the start of a beloved poem by the English poet William Blake (1757–1827). The rhythm, the alliterations, and the metaphors at hand—the possibilities—will be immediately felt.

The Tyger

*Ty*ger! *Ty*ger! *burn*ing *bright*
In the *for*ests of the *night*,
What im*mor*tal *hand* or *eye*
Could *frame* thy *fear*ful *sym*metry?
In what *dis*tant *deeps* or *skies*
Burnt the *fire* of *thine eyes*?
On what *wings* dare *he* as*pire*?

What does the hand dare *seize* the *fire*?[16]

High-level poetry's vividness and resources are immeasurable—and sound is an inherent part of the metaphor. Because both the poet and the gifted analyst work deeply in metaphors, frequent visits to that vast universe of poetry can enhance the therapist's practice by bringing new music, rhythm, and embodiment. A resource that can be valuable both to the therapist who has had rare encounters with poetic expression and the one who has developed a deep love affair with poetry.

In *The Making of a Poem*, for instance, Mark Strand and Eavan Boland can supply the reader with the richness of verse forms, revealing meter, voice, and so much more than the analyst can look at not as locks but valuable keys to keep him alert to the music of the emotionally alive therapeutic dialogue.[17]

In fact, in the preface of his book *Best Words, Best Order*, the American poet and novelist Stephen Dobyns says:

> A work of literature is something made by the writer that is meant to move the heart of a reader. Let's add to this William Carlos Williams's remark: "If it ain't a pleasure, it ain't a poem." While this oversimplifies, it is a beginning. It also suggests that writing is a craft, and a craft can be learned. Not everyone can learn it, but if one has imagination, a certain intelligence, the ability to make metaphors, a passion for language, for the world, for communication, as well as a passion for the medium, then usually there is a chance of learning the craft. I believe that a poem is a window that hangs between two or more human beings who otherwise live in darkened rooms.[18]

This is the basic metaphor in the poem "Asphodel, That Greeny Flower," by William Carlos Williams. And it is also part of the reason for the present proliferation of writing workshops, MFAs, and the overall professionalization of poetry. A poem doesn't try to present reality but presents a metaphor that represents some aspect of the writer's relation to the world: a metaphor that can be potentially experienced and becomes meaningful to the reader.

But like in a poem, the truth of our lives doesn't fit into a linear narrative. Dobyns goes further in his remark:

> It can even be argued that it is the reader who makes the poem because if the ideal reader cannot re-create the emotion out of the poet's words, then no poem exists. Likewise, the reader has to be able to make the emotion his or her own. It is not enough for the reader to understand—to be a witness to somebody else's experience. So, it can be said that the poem is not about the writer but the reader and that without this link to the reader, the poem is only a jumble of words.[19]

One could tie Dobyns's remarks to the transformative interpretation that contributes to a client's perception change during analysis.

In another of his books, *Next Word, Better Word*, Dobyns proposes that

> Writing a poem is one of the ways to love the world." . . . In human society art has several definite purposes, and it has served them in every culture going back as far as traces of humankind can be found. By showing us that other human beings can feel exactly as we do, poetry educates our sense of empathy and teaches us to live in a society.[20]

That sense of empathy, that opportunity for insight received through a poem's metaphors, is shown to us by the American poet Marie Howe (1950), who worked as a newspaper reporter and teacher before receiving her MFA from Columbia University in 1983. Marie Howe is one of American poetry's most original and genuinely visionary voices. Her most recent collection, *Magdalene*, imagines the biblical figure of Mary Magdalene as a woman who embodies the spiritual and sensual, alive in a contemporary landscape. We can say that Howe's Magdalene character comes to the contemporary landscape as an archetype.

In an interview for *American Poet*, Howe shares her valued experience with the readers:

> When I was the New York State Poet I was fortunate to collaborate with the MTA Arts and Design team, the Poetry Society of America, the visual artist Gabriel Barcia-Colombo, dozens of other poets, and the public to create *The Poet Is In*, an interactive poetry event we held in Grand Central Terminal and the new Fulton Street transportation hub. The idea originated from the old Peanuts comic—Lucy in a booth offering advice. We created domesticated spaces within a public space by placing poets at desks, with rugs, floor lamps, typewriters, and chairs pulled up to the desks so that people might sit and ask for a poem.
>
> First, the poet and the person talked together. From that conversation, the poet pulled images, dreams, memories, statements, and—in an act of transformation, using words, silence, image, the line—created a poem that gave some of that back to the person. The poet typed on carbon paper and, when finished, pulled the poem out, separated the copies, signed one, read it aloud to the person who had asked for it, then gave it to that person to keep. Most people wept. The poets were so moved that many didn't want to stop when their hour ended. And this is what most surprised us: People waited in line for more than two hours to speak with a poet and to have a poem written for them.[21]

Howe's description shows us how essential it is, in the universal process of psychological transformation, which takes place in the development of the personality over the life course and in analytical psychotherapy, to be validated by another human being. In that case, by a poet through a poem.

She affirms that "The success of *The Poet Is In* is evidence of the hunger for insight and articulated meaning in all of us. It is relational and transformative—people can glimpse how a poem might be made—and it is a gift given, person to poet, poet to person. Each as each: mirrored."[22]

The author connects Howe's remarks about the success of *The Poet Is In* to the empathy that can be developed in the analytical experience. In that situation, a trained and intuitive psychoanalyst can hear the client's trauma, joy, and hope—and bring these vital affective realities to the session as a most profound experience—as a client's life poem.

In that same edition of *American Poet*, Jane Hirshfield, whose poem "Autumn" we've read earlier in this book, offers a few poems as her personal anthology. She says: Any good poem can be, in its rightly matched moment, a reservoir of recalibration, remembrance, restoration of the capacity for joy.[23]

One of the poems she offered is "Postscript" by Seamus Heaney (1939–2013). Widely recognized as one of the major poets of the twentieth century, Heaney, a native of Northern Ireland, received the 1995 Nobel Prize.

The poem's title appears as something added *after* something: a postscript. But it is not. What is being set up in the very opening lines of the poem is related to Hirshfield's definition of poetry as a reservoir of recalibration, remembrance, and joy.

Heaney starts "Postscript" by suggesting to the reader:

> And some time make the time to drive out west
> Into County Clare, along the Flaggy Shore,
> He appears to have the intention to be precise. He says:
> In September or October, when the wind
> And the light are working off each other.

That part of the poem, which can be represented by the wind and the light working off each other, reminds us of the parts of a metaphor. They are working off each other.

Hirshfield comments about that poem that, at first, meandering, conversational, and descriptive, Heaney's advice seems casual, happenstance. But by its end, the poet has applied one of the excellent, unexpected poultices for the broken spirit or heart, stepping beyond the personal into amazement and wonder.[24]

In her comments about that poem, Hirshfield refers to the poet's intention:

> At first meandering, conversational, and descriptive, Heaney's offered advice seems casual, happenstance. But by its end, the poet has applied one of the great, unexpected poultices for the broken spirit or heart: stepping beyond the personal into amazement and wonder.[25]

INTUITION AND NUMINOSITY

Being interviewed for *The Paris Review*, the American poet W. S. Merwin (1927–2019), who wrote more than fifty books, died at ninety-one, and was one of the most highly decorated poets in the nation, was asked: Do you see a connection between poetry and prayer?

Merwin responded:

> I guess the simple answer is yes, if only because I think of poetry as an attempt to use language as completely as possible. And if you want to do that, obviously, you're not concerned with language as decoration or language as amusement, although you certainly want the language to be pleasurable. Pleasure is part of completeness. I think of poetry as having to do with the completeness of life, and the completeness of relation with one's experience, completing one's experience, articulating it, making sense of it.[26]

As we consider intuition and numinosity in poetry, one could connect a remark by the French scientist Teilhard de Chardin (1881–1955) with the poem "For the Anniversary of My Death," composed by Merwin.

The French Jesuit, scientist, paleontologist, theologian, philosopher, and teacher Pierre Teilhard de Chardin worked to understand evolution and faith. He proposed, "Matter is spirit moving slowly enough to be seen."

In the opening lines of his beautiful poem "For the Anniversary of My Death," Merwin establishes a space between a known reality (life) and an unknown space (the beyond.) In that description, the poet calls silence to the front. That's important because silence is part of the death of everybody—but especially for Merwin, whose life—we can say—was built so much on language. The way the poet presents that change suggests that he will also pass like a tireless traveler, the beam of a lightless star:

> Every year, without knowing it, I have passed the day
> when the last fires will wave to me.[27]

In this poem, Merwin focuses on "the completeness of life, and the completeness of relation with one's experience, completing one's experience, articulating it, making sense of it." But he also treats "matter (as) spirit moving slowly enough to be seen."[28]

One could admire the brilliant succession of metaphors and the way the poet describes the transition between being alive and what he imagines as not being conscious of life anymore. He brings to the surface the fact that we live each day of our lives, year after year, without being able to notice which of these days will be, later on, associated with our death. A numinous reality that is—consciously or unconsciously—the inheritance of all creation.

In fact, Jung famously said that

> The main interest of my work is not concerned with treating neurosis but rather with the approach to the numinous. The fact is that the approach to the numinous is the real therapy, and since you attain the numinous experiences, you are released from the curse of pathology. Even the very disease takes on a numinous character.[29]

The numinous metaphor, as in Merwin's poem—reminding the reader that each day of the year could be the day of his death, to be celebrated one year later—can also direct the reader's attention to human impermanence. That poignancy—also present in the following Stephen Dobyns poem, can again remind us of some intuitive, numinous metaphors analysts have witnessed in the analytical relationship with clients.

Dobyns, an American poet, and novelist, born in 1941, who has published over a dozen volumes of poetry, honors a deceased friend in "Good Days." He starts by summarizing a good day with friends around a bonfire, telling stories—a circle of light within the dark. At the end of his poem, he suggests that "As time passed, one by one, men and women got to their feet and walked into the night."[30]

Of course, the reader can immediately recognize these "men and women who, one by one, got to their feet and walked into the night" as a metaphor for the ones who have died—resulting in the poet's sadness. Which, in turn, affects the reader.

In fact, like in the analytical hour, the numinous metaphor can surface at any moment with full power, as it does in the poem "Stillbirth" by Laure-Anne Bosselaar, a Belgian American poet (1943), translator, professor, and former poet laureate of Santa Barbara, California.

Taking advantage of the repetitions required by the pantoum form, Laure-Anne's expressive poem brings to the present metaphor the sounds of despair connected to an event that happened thirty-two years before.

> On a platform, I heard someone call out your name: "*No, Laetitia, no.*"[31]
> The poet describes how this was not her train, but the name she heard made her miss the child she never had.
> It wasn't my train—the doors were closing,[32]

Laetitia was the name the poet had chosen for the child she was expecting. That name means, in Latin, joy. The pronoun "you" brings Laetitia closer to the reader. And the poem is, in a sense, a platform, from where the poet shares with the readers her mourning. The repetition, due to the pantoum form, increases the grief.

WITNESS AND CLOSURE

In contradistinction to human impermanence, a successful poem is transcendent—it does not end.

Stephen Dobyns, in his book *Next Word, Better Word*, says:

> In human affairs, the word "closure" means putting something behind us; in a successful poem, it can mean the invocation of something ahead.
>
> This apparent paradox points to one of a poem's greatest strengths. The poem doesn't end; rather, it gives back meaning with each re-reading.
>
> A lyric poem is a symbol of affective life, the realm of feelings. It was written because the poet has experienced an emotion about which he or she was unable to remain silent. The poet bears witness to that emotion and attempts to recreate it in the reader by presenting pertinent information equally in form and content. That act of bearing witness is what draws us to the poem as readers.
>
> However, the poet must do more than bear witness to an emotional dynamic, which is why the poet Philip Larkin said that "the poem must be theatrical in operation. If the poet is writing because he or she is unable to remain silent, we expect the strength of that emotion to energize the poem. In the making of the poem, that emotion is translated into the poem's theatrical dynamic. This doesn't mean that the poem must be loud, but it must live up to the promise of its speaking.[33]

In his book *Next Word, Better Word*, and considering "closure," Dobyns addresses the state of invocation of something ahead, which remains after the reader gets to the last line of a good poem. He says:

> The poem as a symbol shares a symbol's characteristics: it is nondiscursive; it is a product of the right brain; it is more than the sum of its parts, and it usually presents its information through sense data. In a poem, unlike an anecdote, the reader's question—"What does this mean?"—is not fully answered by its syntactic closure. We have a sense of more, and so we move past the syntactic closure to reread the poem in search of the scope of that "more." But no matter how much we reread; the poem continues to defy paraphrase. It remains dynamic, a living thing. Like any successful symbol, it continues to give back information, to transmit meaning.
>
> So, in that particular "absence of an ending," one could say that a good poem is like a successful, deep Jungian analysis. Analysis can be stopped, but the process never ends.[34]

The reader can witness that poetic closure principle at work in "A Moment," a poem by the American poet Kurt Brown (1944–2013). Brown, who founded the Aspen Writers' Conference, and taught at Sarah Lawrence College and Georgia Institute of Technology, published many books of and about poetry.

The end line of Brown's poem "and I recalled myself and smiled back" executes precisely that turning back to the beginning. In fact, the poet was doing that "rereading" for us since the first line when he shared: "I keep returning to that moment, one."[35] And "one" at the end of that first line is a powerful line break, which intensifies the reader's attention for that *one* crucial moment. The reader stops there. It is a "here and now" like the one we deal with in our work as psychoanalysts.

> I keep returning to that moment, one
> Day at your kitchen table[36]

Following Brown's poem, which points to a specific, dramatic moment, we can transition to another poem where another specific and significant moment is brought to the reader's attention through a vivid metaphor. The poem I have in mind is "Two Countries," by the poet Naomi Shihab Nye's (1952), who gives voice to her experience as an Arab American writer through powerful poems about heritage and peace overflowing with a humanitarian spirit.

In her poem, the poet shares the trauma of a highly evolved person who is not recognized as a valued human being in a foreign country. The metaphor—told to the reader by her skin—proposes that she is like a bird's feather lost, swept away by someone who never saw it was a feather. The feather of an awe-inspiring singing bird, the reader could conclude. The title of the poem is "Two Countries."

> Even now, when skin is not alone,
> It remembers being alone and thanks something.[37]

Considering the two last lines of Naomi's poem—"that people go places larger than themselves," and to amplify our discussion on witness and closure—one could quote what Ada Limón (1976), an American poet who authored six poetry books and won the National Book Critics Circle Award for Poetry, said in an interview to *The Writer's Chronicle* in 2019.

In that text, titled *Naming the Animal*, the interviewer asked: "How do you cultivate a balance of wildness and a finished piece?"

Limón responded: "My main rule is to follow the poem. . . . It's one of my favorite things about writing; I never know what's going to happen."[38]

As psychoanalysts, I think that we profoundly agree with the poet's observation. In our practice as well—where, sometimes, we must ride dragons, as described by Robert Bly in *Leaping Poetry*—the process wants to go someplace that most likely will surprise us. And that's one of our favorite things about the work.

NOTES

1. Jung, C. G. *Collected Works* (Princeton, NJ: Princeton University Press, 1969), 82, 88–113, 129, 321, 323.
2. Hirshfield, Jane. "Autumn" (*The Paris Review*, issue 109).
3. Jung, C. G. *Collected Works* (Princeton, NJ: Princeton University Press, 1944), 130, 148, 400.
4. Ibid.
5. Bly, Robert. *Leaping Poetry* (Pittsburgh, PA: University of Pittsburgh Press, 2008), 4.
6. Ibid.
7. Ibid
8. Sze, Arthur. "Sleepers." (Academy of American Poets, 2019).
9. Vivona, J. M. "Embracing Figures of Speech: The Transformative Potential of Spoken Language" (*Psychoanalytic Psychology* 20, no. 1, 2003).
10. Ibid.
11. Williams, W. C. "Asphodel, That Greeny Flower.*" Pictures from Brueghel and Other Poems* (New York: New Directions, 1962), 153–82.
12. Hillman, J. *Re-Visioning Psychology* (New York: Harper & Row, 1975), 156.
13. Bass, E. *Conversation between Ellen Bass and Alan Fox* (*Rattle* 40, 2013): 1–7.
14. Edinger, E. *The Eternal Drama: The Inner Meaning of Greek Mythology* (Boston: Shambhala Publications, Inc., 1994), 83.
15. Ibid.
16. Blake, William. "The Tyger" (The Poetry Foundation, 2023).
17. Strand, M., and E. Boland (eds.). *The Making of a Poem: A Norton Anthology of Poetic Forms* (London: W.W. Norton & Company Ltd., 2001).
18. Dobyns, S. *Best Words, Best Order: Essays on Poetry* (New York: Palgrave Macmillan, 2003), xii, 5.
19. Ibid.
20. Dobyns, S. *Next Word, Better Word: The Craft of Writing Poetry* (New York: Palgrave Macmillan, 2011), 147–48.
21. Howe, M., and Nick Patrick. "Backchat: Marie Howe in Conversation" (*American Poet* 54, Spring–Summer edition, 2018).
22. Ibid.
23. Hirshfield, Jane. "Poetry, Permeability, and Healing" (Academy of American Poets, 2023), 1–2.
24. Heaney, S. "Postscript." *Opened Ground: Selected Poems 1966–1996* (New York: Farrar, Straus and Giroux, 1998).
25. Hirshfield, Jane. "Poetry, Permeability, and Healing" (Academy of American Poets, 2023), 1–2.

26. Ibid.
27. Ibid.
28. Ibid.
29. Jung, C. G. *Collected Works* (Princeton NJ: Princeton University Press, 1944), 130, 148, 400.
30. Dobyns, S. "Good Days." *The Day's Last Light Reddens the Leaves of the Copper Beech* (Rochester, NY: BOA Editions Ltd., 2016).
31. Bosselaar, L. A. "Stillbirth." *A New Hunger*. (Keene, NY: Ausable Press, 2007).
32. Ibid.
33. Dobyns, S. *Next Word, Better Word: The Craft of Writing Poetry* (New York: Palgrave Macmillan, 2011), 147–48.
34. Ibid.
35. Brown, K. "A Moment" (*The Cortland Review,* 2014): 1.
36. Ibid.
37. Nye, N. S. "Two Countries." *From Words Under the Words: Selected Poems* (New York: Far Corner, 1995).
38. Limón, A. "Naming the Animal" (*The Writer's Chronicle*, 2019): 17.

Chapter 6

The Green Sandal of Cinderella

Metaphor and Individuation in Fairy Tales

As one focuses on metaphors and symbols in fairy tales, one can discover how useful they are to analytical psychology as tools at the disposal of analysts and students of Jungian analysis when working with clients.

Verena Kast, in the foreword of her book *The Dynamics of Symbols*, says that "Creativity is central to C. G. Jung's psychology. The goal of Jungian therapy is that individuals begin to experiment with their reality and creatively deal with their problems and personal traits. Neuroses are to be replaced by the potential of creative change. Creative development becomes visible in symbols and is presented to consciousness by symbols."[1]

Fairy tales work like a mirror to the reader and communities in the stories they have described worldwide for thousands of years. That's the reason one can look at them as metaphors.

Working with symbols forms the core of Jungian therapy, and fairy tales characterize Jungian therapy as compared to other methods. Fairy tales are frequently used in typical Jungian analysis, which is one reason they are presented to the reader in this book about metaphor and symbols.

Dr. Kast points out, in her book *The Dynamics of Symbols:*

> Jungian psychology offers the techniques necessary to make the creative potential of the unconscious accessible to consciousness and thereby transform possibility into actuality. These "techniques" are essential in an individual's therapy, both for psychic development toward autonomy and for the development of a creative lifestyle, which in turn will lead the individual to realize that his or her problems are relative not only to the environment shared with others but also to his or her personal depth. By taking the manifestations of both sides seriously, the individual can develop creative solutions that will be expressions of her or his vital self.[2]

One could call this client's personal work Individuation.

The name Cinderella derives from the word *cinders*—ashes. The story of her flexible persona and feminine individuation emerges from glowing embers in over seven hundred versions. The fairy tale has been told—from China to Africa, to Europe, to the Americas—and some of these slightly different tales reach back in time as much as a thousand years.

As we focus on the symbols fairy tales present, one could be reminded of Pech-Merle, the cave discovered by two teenagers in 1922. That's the place where prehistoric artists stretched out their hands toward the wall and blew red ochre and black cinder over them, leaving their signature visible to us 20,000 years later. These hands and the astounding animal paintings surrounding them may attest to the persistent human effort toward consciousness and the timeless human dedication to symbolic images.

In this chapter, prior writings by Jung and others on the concept of the symbol will be presented, as well as considerations on the concept of persona—which may regulate the relationship between the inner and outside world in the development of individuation, as well as a briefly comment on the Grimms' version of Cinderella and an interpretation of two personal dreams. One could say that, from the point of view of this chapter, the changing of the shoe (a symbol of the individual footprint and the person's standing point) in this fairy tale is even more important than the change of dresses.

The author's interest in the Cinderella fairy tale emerged from a significant personal dream connected with the topic. That first dream was followed sixteen months later by a related one that involved synchronicity. Before those two dreams, which will be described later, the author had no specific interest in the Cinderella story and knew only Perrault's version. Given that these two dreams had surprised her, she was eager to attend a class taught by Dr. Elisabeth Grözinger at the C. G. Jung Institute. The title of Grözinger's presentation was "Cinderella as a Story of Female Individuation."[3]

The presenter called the class's attention to the relevance of the fairy tale, which, when read by men, can bring awareness about the anima's insight and, when read by women, can illuminate the practical function of the animus. The story may also powerfully contribute to the present world's necessity for relationships. Beyond the suspicion of narcissism versus hope for a relationship, Dr. Grözinger emphasized the importance of Cinderella's feminine persona—as a connection between the ego and the outside world—and the flexibility displayed in the tale, her ability to adapt when surrounded by shadowy circumstances, as well as her anxiety for independence and openness to receive joy.[4]

THE SYMBOL AS MEDIATOR

Liliane Frey-Rohn, in her comparative study "From Freud to Jung," says that one of Jung's most remarkable insights was the concept of the symbol as a mediator, unifying the opposites of conscious and unconscious. She points out that "The symbol was an image which, on the one hand, was a manifestation of the primordial psychic background not yet rationally shaped and, on the other hand, participated in conscious reality. Jung saw the symbol as a paradoxical expression, aiming at the unification of the Yea and the Nay and encompassing both."[5]

Every psychic product, if it is the best possible expression at the moment for a fact as yet unknown or only relatively known, may be regarded as a symbol. For that reason, a dream, as well as a fairy tale, is a symbol that, in its journey to us, may serve as a vessel containing other symbols.

Jung used the concept of symbol according to the Greek etymology: *sym*/connect, unite; *balein*/toward an objective. *Symbalein*, in ancient Greece, meant the act of joining two halves of one thing, like a coin or a shelf, which had been slashed when two individuals departed from each other. When, later on, one of these two friends wanted to send an urgent message to the other, the messenger would bring with him the other half of the coin, for example. In this way, the person who would receive the message could verify the perfect union of the two halves: one known, the other unknown.

The word "symbol" started to be used to designate the union of two opposites: something conscious—known—with something unconscious—unknown. Because that which is unknown has an affective value, the symbol always brings about emotion. Here is the numinous aspect of the symbol: it points to a connection between the conscious and the unconscious dimensions of the same phenomenon. Even when one rationally knows the design and colors of a flag, for instance, it is difficult not to feel emotion when one sees it waving at a major international event. Thus, the symbol represents the connection with the energy needed to produce events that alter things.

Symbols surface from the archetypal depths of the personality, the collective unconscious, and build a bridge between the conscious and the unconscious. The ego does not invent them. Jung says, in his essay on "Psychic Energy" under the title *Symbol Formation,* that "The psychological mechanism that transforms energy is the symbol. I mean by this a real symbol and not a sign."[6]

Indeed, signs can be seen and understood without loss of meaning—an image inside a building indicating the way to the stairways is a sign, not a symbol. In contrast, a real symbol emerges out of the numinous and opens one up to mystery.

Paul Tillich, for instance, proposes that "the symbol grows from the ground up," and maintains that a living symbol can reveal hidden levels of meaning and transcendent or religious realities. For Tillich, a symbol always "points beyond itself" to something that is unquantifiable and mysterious: the symbol's "depth dimension." The unique nature of a symbol, Tillich says, is that it gives access to deeper layers of reality that are otherwise inaccessible.[7]

Mircea Eliade, a renowned researcher in the area of the psychology of religion, mythology, and magic, argues in his study *Images and Symbols* that "The ethnologist of today has not only grasped the importance of symbolism in archaic thinking but has seen its intrinsic coherence, its validity, its speculative audacity, its "nobility." He adds: "The greatest merit of C. G Jung is that he has gone further than Freudian psychoanalysis on the plane of psychology itself and has thus restored the spiritual significance of the image."[8]

Indeed, symbols contain elements of spirit and instinct, image and drive—and are the great organizers of libido. The reason that symbols have such importance for Jung derives from their ability to *transform natural energy into cultural and spiritual forms.* In his essay "On Psychic Energy," Jung provides a formal theoretical account of transformations and appears extremely interested in how these changes occur.[9] In fact, a fundamental distinction between the theories of Jung and Freud—*and the reason for the end of their collaboration*—resides in the difference between *transformation* and *sublimation.*

Freud believed that humans could sublimate libidinal desires—but that resulting sublimation would constitute a mere substitute for the real objects of that desire. From that point of view, the libido would always be wishing to return to the respective mother, father, and childhood, to Oedipal fantasies. Freudian analysis, thus, would be continuously reductive.

In contrast, Jung posits that, whereas the infant's libido originally seeks the mother's body, due to its necessity for survival, later on, the libido will flow through other gradients—into procreation, in adulthood, for example. When the libido encounters an image analogue, a spiritual metaphor, though, it will go in that direction, not because this is a substitute for sexual desire, but because it is its intrinsic goal to do so.[10]

For Jung, this is a transformation of libido, now a desexualized libido, and culture is created from such transformations—like in the case of a gorgeous poem, the music composed for an oboe, a delicious dinner at an excellent restaurant, the work that organizations like Médicins Sans Frontières accomplish, etc.

Jung believes that human nature leads to culture formation, to the creation of symbols, to the containment of energy so that its flow can be directed toward these spiritual and mental contents. The tension between the archetype and instinct in the symbol is what makes the symbol alive.[11]

INTERPRETATION OF CINDERELLA: A STORY OF FEMININE INDIVIDUATION

Edward Edinger, in "Ego and Archetype," argues that,

> in contrast to the abstract, objective meanings conveyed by signs, there is another kind of meaning, namely subjective, a living meaning which does not refer to abstract knowledge but rather to a psychological state which can affirm life. One could use this sense of the word when describing a deeply moving experience as something meaningful. Such an experience does not convey an abstract meaning, at least not primarily, but a rather living meaning which, laden with affect, relates one organically to life as a whole. Dreams, myths, and works of art can convey this sense of subjective, living meaning, which differs from objective, abstract meaning.[12]

Reading the story of Cinderella, the female heroine in the Grimms' version, one could find himself or herself experiencing this living meaning which relates us organically to life as a whole.

Research has shown that there are over seven hundred known versions of the fairy tale generated by different authors worldwide. Grimm's version was first published at the beginning of 1800. Another well-known version, created by Charles Perrault, was used as a basis for Disney's film adaptation. In terms of psychic maturity, it acts significantly differently from the one just considered.

In the Grimms' tale, Cinderella invests a lot of creativity to obtain her liberation and shows a healthy anxiety for independence from the constraints of her milieu. In contrast, in Perrault's version, the godmother greatly helps her, blesses her abundantly, and brings horses and carriages to serve her.

Perrault's version is more appropriate to be read by people who still have a small ego—individuals in the first half of life, for example. When confronted with the painful events restricting her development, the wisdom and maturity of the Grimms' character are better understood and integrated by readers individuating in the second half of life.

Indeed, one of the fundamental psychological contributions of Cinderella in the Grimms' version is her development of individuation. She also contributes a juicy, flexible example as a resourceful persona. The Jungian concept of persona can be seen as a social skin: it is that psychic interface between the ego and society that makes up one's social identity in the outside world. In this story, the persona appears symbolized by the gorgeous dresses and the remarkable shoes. One could interpret clothes and shoes more specifically later. Let us turn first to individuation and relationships.

One of the essential concepts in Jungian psychology is the process of *individuation.* It describes the psychic development that leads to the conscious awareness of wholeness. Jung's evolutive psychology traces the individuation process along the entire human evolution—at the personal and collective levels. That process, which results from the interaction between the individual and the collective, aims at allowing one to become who she or he really is—manifesting one's potential powerfully. Given that the *process of individuation* will happen all through a person's life—i.e., the ego will be continuously structured by archetypal symbols—the Jungian clinical practice is extensively based on working with symbols.

The interpretation of symbols, either on a subjective or an objective level, comes from the belief that individuation includes both integration and relationship. Indeed, Jung argues that the "relationship to the self is at once relationship to our fellow man, and no one can be related to the latter until he is related to himself."[13]

From this point of view, Cinderella shows us how deeply she is connected to the good in her. This is true even when her stepsisters and stepmother deprive her of all of her beautiful dresses and personal effects, clad her in an old gray bed-gown, mock her, and send her to the kitchen to work for them from morning till night. They even manage—apparently through their trickster behavior—to make Cinderella's father *forget* that she is *also* one of his daughters.

Despite all the misery surrounding her, Cinderella can still manifest her resourcefulness. In addition to laboring in the kitchen—that essential, symbolic space where significant transformation happens—she finds a place of refuge near the little tree she has planted by her mother's grave. There, the white bird and other sky creatures stand for the spirit of the departed. They help her. That hideaway in nature, with plants and trees, represents the Self—the center and source of innate psychic tendencies toward structure, order, and integration—the source of wholeness.

Another characteristic of Cinderella is that she is modest. She clearly discerns that she will not be able to accomplish the heroic tasks the stepmother commands her to do by herself—and *asks for help*, *which* allows help to come from wherever help is.

On the other hand, the stepsisters and stepmother appear to be good candidates to symbolize another side of the individuation process: the shadow. In Jung's thought, the shadow comprises the rejected and unaccepted aspects of the personality that are repressed. These elements form a compensatory structure opposing the ego's self-ideals and the persona.

Ann and Barry Ulanov, in their study *Cinderella and Her Sisters: The Envied and the Envying*, look at Perrault's version from the point of view of envy, which they say in the preface "is an emotion we all know about scholars, psychoanalysts, and theologians included, but we rarely talk about it, and very little is written about it. But envy exists and works its destruction, all the more successfully because we refuse to face it."[14]

In essence, they affirm, envy is an attack on being—the being of the envied and of the envier, too—and an attack on the good quality or stuff that is envied. If we refuse to talk about our experiences of envy, we conspire with its savage attempts to annihilate the good, anything that is in any way good, however we define it. Finally, envy between persons is a displacement of our own relation to the good. When Cinderella's sisters envy her, they get off the hook of their struggle with themselves and their relation to the good. They dodge to relate to their own selves by means of noisy accusations directed against Cinderella. They avoid figuring out their relation—to their mother, the prince, or what they see as the good life. Instead of inspecting and muddling along in these real relationships, they mount vociferous attacks on Cinderella. All the sisters' energies go into trying to destroy Cinderella's being instead of trying to take hold of their own, sexually and spiritually.[15]

In the same convoluted way, one could add, as she announces the heroic tasks Cinderella must accomplish before being allowed to go to the ball, the stepmother behaves like *she* is the source of Being, the source of all good things—but she is not. The Ulanovs emphasize:

> If we can suffer envy consciously, we ourselves feel whether coming from us or at us, it can be a means of recovering being for us. Envy can lead us to what needs repair in our identities, in our sexuality and our spiritual centers, and in our efforts to relate to the good. And envy can point us toward the very good that undergirds both the pain and the healing. Envy, that great distance maker, that connection destroyer, can, if suffered consciously, close the gap that its own wounding operations have opened.[16]

The analysis by Ann and Barry Ulanov can, of course, be applied to the stepsisters and stepmother in the Grimms' story as well as to other versions, given that, as a rule, all these characters—who represent some aspects of the shadow—"out of envy, try to steal the good as the only possible way to possess it and yet keep it at a safe distance."[17]

In contrast, Cinderella, when the prince is finally able to recognize her—which happens only after he had almost brought each stepsister with him to the castle to marry them because he had failed to see that the person he was taking along was not the one with whom he had danced all evening for three times—Cinderella embraces the joy that comes to her with all her heart and is ready for the conjunction.

In fact, in Jung's thought, the *anima*—the feminine insight that Cinderella represents for men reading this version—and the *animus*—the prince, bringing with him a practical system of evaluation for women—are the royal way between the ego and the deepest layer of the psyche, the self.

The Liberator prince in this story, by the way, is not sufficiently aggressive and needed the pigeons/good mother to call his attention to the fact that, in his first two attempts, the footprint within the shoe of the one he was carrying with him did not belong to the "real bride." Both times, though, he listened and turned back—a good sign that he could pay attention to the feminine advice.

Feet connects the individual to earth and, in repeated steps, to the ground of reality. Cinderella calls our attention to her representation of a persona, grounded and resourceful, flexible, and determined to discern—like picking out lentils from the ashes—the elements that could be useful to her.

In Jungian psychology, the concept of persona gets its name from the mask used by the actors in the Greek theater. As previously defined, the persona arises from the need to adapt to life and society to its social constraints. Our personal type of mask can be collectively accepted and recognized. The persona is responsible for our adaptability to the social world. It expresses itself in our lifestyle, the profession we practice, how we interact with our friends, how we dress, and the shoes we choose. It is certainly true that, in Jungian tradition, people pay more attention to animus and anima. But the persona is essential because it regulates the relationship between the inner and outer world. The persona is not only an external element but *an entrance to the ego.*

In this fairy tale, the flexibility of Cinderella's persona is represented in the change of clothes, from the old gray bed-gown and the wooden shoes used in the kitchen to the beautiful dresses obtained to go to the ball in the castle and, of course, to the pivotal shoes. Indeed, one can enjoy having several personae, and it is a significant decision to discern at what moment to "change dresses" to better use our talents in a given situation.

That's a task for all of us: we must be able to assign the right aspect of our persona to the right place in our lives.

When, in contrast, the persona is extremely rigid, it can break from the deeper dimensions of the self and turn into a mere representation of a desired external point without reflecting the depths of the ontological personal self. When organically integrated, though, the persona might turn into a very creative element that allows the expression of different facets of the individual. As a tool for adaptation, the persona brings great potential for change. Cinderella's persona, thus, regulates the relationship between the inner and the outside world during the development of her feminine individuation. Because the individual footprint is extremely personal, representing her standpoint in her life, the change of shoes is even more important than the change of dresses.

Functioning as the animus, the prince can honor her in her femininity. He admires her in her individuation—"This is my partner," he says to those who want to dance with her—and allows her to show her full beauty to everybody in the world. In fact, the story of Cinderella, in Grimm's version, is particularly necessary for our world today in terms of contributing to the necessity of relationships.

On the other side of the archetype, and in contrast to the prince, Cinderella's father appears aggressive: he slashes the pigeon house to pieces, chops the pear tree down, and *forgets* that Cinderella is his only real daughter. He remembered to bring her the hazel twig, though—the branch of the hazel bush she planted at her mother's grave and characterizes her growing relationship with Nature and with herself, the development of her journey to individuation.

Regarding the doves and pigeons' symbol, one could say that, since cave-dwelling times, people have been fascinated by these celestial creatures believed to embody sacred forces. Great-mother goddesses of love and fecundity like Babylonian Ishtar, Phoenician Atargatis, and Greek Aphrodite took the form of a dove. Rome's love goddess, Venus is also connected to doves. Innocence, beauty, peace, and simplicity are also attributes of doves. The Song of Solomon 2:4 reads: "O my dove, in the clefts of the rock, / in the covert of the cliff, / let me see your face, / let me hear your voice,/ for your voice is sweet,/ and your face is comely."[18]

With a soft voice and sovereign adaptability, Cinderella reminds us that all human production, like music, is based on a factor that transcends matter and consciousness: the symbol, an indispensable element in the evolution of humanity and culture. In summary, Cinderella appears to be integrating persona and shadow—as polarities of the ego—by fully accepting these parts that do not belong in the persona image, being receptive to her own nature, and being open to wholeness. Her archetypal image as a feminine heroine teaches us how to acquire new abilities and conquer hurdles apparently unsurmountable. Her open-minded character helps readers trust in the transcendent and transitory aspects of the human condition, while the symbols in the story function as facilitating elements in the integration of unconscious contents.

INTERPRETATION OF A FIRST DREAM: *WHY IS MY NAME CINDERELLA OF ALL FLOWERS?*

The author of this book had just arrived in Honolulu, Hawaii, to attend a conference there when, in the evening, she had the following dream:

In the dream, she is with a friend on a street during daylight. Only the two of them are there. They are standing on the sidewalk, and the author's friend, standing to her right side, is wearing a beautiful, elegant, long white dress embroidered in white and pleated with delicate folds at the hem. She looks intently at the author and asks:

- Why is my name "Cinderella of All Flowers?"

The author looks at her with the same focused attention and replies:

- You are the one who should tell me why your name is Cinderella of All Flowers.

The one who asked the question pauses and appears to ponder the author's response. Then, she turns to her left and crosses the street to the other side diagonally (toward the right), walking on the cobblestones that pave the street.

Maria José had been the author's close and dear lifelong friend. The author was concerned about her because she was very ill in Brazil at the time. One could interpret that the dream could have given the author an objective hint (which had happened to her a few times regarding other people) about her departure to the beyond. Indeed, in the dream, she crossed the street to the other side, and the fact that the road was paved with cobblestones reminded the author of certain streets in the interior of Brazil.

The following morning, the author called her friend's daughter to see how she was doing. The author's friend was in the same situation, but nothing significant had happened to her. So, the author was relieved and worked on the dream only from the subjective point of view of her personal life. She liked Hawaii, had visited the state several times, beautiful flowers grew there, and she was married in Maui. She thought this was a dream related to her second half of life, and how she would cross that street.

SECOND DREAM: THE GREEN SANDAL OF CINDERELLA

Sixteen months later, the author had just arrived in Brazil for the holidays and, with her husband, went to Búzios, a lovely beach a couple of hours from Rio, to celebrate their wedding anniversary. She had planned to visit Maria José a few days later, when she would go back to Rio, but had not talked to her yet. On the evening preceding December 16, she had the following dream:

> She sees her own right hand extended and, resting in its palm, she sees the right foot of a delicate, beautiful green sandal. The color green in that sandal was exceptionally beautiful and lively.

The following morning, the author was meditating, remembering that dream and pondered: Why is there only one foot of the sandal? What could this mean? And then, suddenly, she remembered the dream she had had in Honolulu, where Maria José asked, "Why is my name Cinderella of All Flowers?" Of course, she thought: Cinderella! The one whom we recognize due to that one shoe she leaves behind. And then she deeply wished that the dream would not be intuitively telling her that Maria José had departed.

That evening, December 16, while the author was having dinner with her husband, to celebrate their anniversary, her phone rang. It was Maria José's daughter. She told the author that her mother had passed away early that morning, while in an ambulance, on her way to the hospital. The author asked her when this happened and realized that she had had the dream with the green sandal exactly when Maria José was crossing the street to the beyond.

The family asked the author to sing Maria José's Mass, which she did accompanied by organ and violin. Afterward, several people shared with her that they were glad about the music pieces she had chosen. They brought them a feeling of joy. She pondered silently: Yes, like the vibrant green color of the sandal left behind, like the flowering of herself in the first dream.

INTERPRETATION OF THE ARMLESS MAIDEN: A TRADITIONAL RUSSIAN STORY

Fairy tales are very useful to students of analytical psychology. Some stories have existed for centuries, have been studied all over the world, and have been carefully classified. They can be excellent tools at the disposal of the practitioner in the analysis of clients. In the continuation of this chapter, the author will present a few examples of fairy tales' metaphors, which show the richness and significance of Jungian vision for a deeper understanding of the multidimensional picture of the unconscious.

The Type

Checking "The Types of the Folktale, a Classification, and Bibliography," by Anti Aarne and the following authors, the general type of this Fairy Tale is number 706, listed as The Maiden Without Hands. In the fairy tale we are considering—which belongs to the more general series "The Banished Wife or Maiden"—the heroine, in summary, (I) has her arms (hands, in the classification) cut off by her brother, who was tricked by the rivalry of his wife against her sister. (II) The son of a rich merchant couple (a king, in the classification) meets her and marries her despite of her mutilation. (III) The heroine also represents The Calumniated Wife type, who is cast off with her newborn child because of the substitution of letters produced by the sister-in-law. (IV) A miracle restores her hands, and she is received again by her husband.[19]

One can associate *The Maiden Without Hands* to the general category 450, *Little Brother and Little Sister*, where brother and sister escape together, and the brother is transformed by the cruel stepmother—in this case, his wife—into a roe or a sheep. Rather a sheep in this story, given that he is not able to see evil, believes her machinations and acts in accordance. In the end, the villain receives the punishment she has unwittingly suggested by attacking not only other humans but by decapitating a horse: the brother attaches her to the tail of his best mare and lets it run in the open field.

Another tale that can be associated with *The Maiden Without Arms* is *Hans my Hedgehog,* type 441, where a childless woman gives birth to a hedgehog. In that tale, the letter written by the sister-in-law says the heroine has given birth to a half-dog and half-bear. In this story, though, the father has a better heart than Hedgehog's father—he burst into tears and writes that his son shall not be molested until he returns. "When I come back," he says, "I will see what kind of baby it is." One could also be reminded of *The Devil with Three Golden Hairs*, type 461, where, as in other tales, letters are captured and substituted by falsified messages (written by the envious king and substituted by the robbers who pitied the hero, for example) to serve their purposes.

The type of fairy tale expressed in *The Maiden Without Arms*, or variations of it can be found in the following cultures: Russian, Finnish, Estonian, Livonian, Lithuanian, Swedish, Danish, Icelandic, Scottish, Irish, French, Spanish, Catalan, Flemish, German, Austrian, Italian, Tuscan, Sicilian, Rumanian, Hungarian, Czech, Slovenian, Serbo-Croatian, Polish, Greek, Turkish, Indian, West Indies, Cape Verde Islands, and other African countries.

One could examine the development of this fairy tale following four phases, as suggested by Verena Kast in "Witches, Ogres, and the Devil's Daughter": Initial situation, intensification, turning point, and concluding situation.

Initial situation: This is the existing condition that brings about the story, to begin with.

What we first learn is that the children's father was a wealthy merchant, and the father and mother died. So, there was no problem in terms of the family's economic situation. The problem is that the father and mother died, and thus, both the warmth and guidance of feminine and masculine models are missing. We might consider whether either child had lived out their Oedipal relationship—particularly for the brother, who seeks a wife who became a negative mother. In any case, we can see the children, in terms of the fairy tale, as abandoned children. This is the reason the brother tells his sister that they will leave (the situation of abandonment.)

The brother has a masculine attitude; he will rent a shop, trade, and find lodgings for his sister. There is a potential problem in this situation, though: "We will live together," he says. The direction of development would ask that they go separate ways or find alternatives. But in that psychological level where they have been "abandoned" and traumatized by the absence of father and mother in their development, it is understandable that they want to live together—supposedly protecting each other. But one could see that the brother is not mature enough to protect himself and his sister from the world's shadow. And she is obedient to him, the male. She believes (or needs to believe) that she can count on him and his discernment.

One could also consider the state of the community where they live. It seems that this wealthy merchant's society (the brother rents a shop and trades, and the future husband of the heroine will also meet her near the wealthy merchants' parents' house) is a sensate society, as a merchants' culture would be expected to be. The brother has learned that young maidens "always take a long time to dress." In fact, the heroine takes time to prepare to go to "the midnight Mass" (for serious reasons, of course, she is afraid, but more about that in a moment), and she gives a sensate observation when her brother tells her to disentangle the carriage: "I cannot do that, she says, I will dirty my dress." She does not claim that she has no strength to disentangle the carriage—she says that she will dirty her dress, which is also symbolic of the trauma and all the suffering she is about to go through. In fact, the heroine is the one who will demonstrate a lot of strength in "disentangling the carriage" of the characters in that story, battling to advance in her own difficult individuation and produce an enlightened work of redemption all around. Throughout the development of the story, the reader can see the significant spiritual and psychological evolution of the girl. In the beginning, she is reluctant to dirty the dress of her persona, and, in the end, accepts her challenging shadow, appearing as a beggar woman through whose young baby we could see the light of the Spirit of God who has guided her.

There is also a word to be said about this community regarding how they treat their women. After telling the heroine to get out and disentangle the carriage, the brother cuts off the girl's arms to the elbows, strikes his horse with the whip, and drives away, abandoning her to her destiny and her unconscious (the woods). The inner reality is that the heroine is abandoned to her own shadow and will be a shadow character for much of her evolution until she is redeemed, at the end.

The brother is also sadistic when he tells her, "I will buy you a new dress, sister, a better one than this"—just before cutting her arms. As a matter of fact, due to the spiritual synchronicities in this archetypal tale and the fruitfulness of her interiority, she will get rewarded with a much better dress than the brother would ever be able to buy! One could also see his violence when disappointed at how much he has acted as an unconscious sheep under the shadow and rage of his wife. He takes his best mare, (a strong female animal, a symbol of fertility) from the stable, ties his wife to its tail, and let it run in the open field until the mare only brings back the braid of the sorcerer. This ties together two opposite forces: the hair of the mare (vigorous instinct, related to Demeter and the earth principle) and the braid of the devil Medusa, who is destroyed.

One could also look at the violence of the brother's wife. To take revenge on her sister-in-law, and appoint her as guilty, she breaks all the furniture in the house (furniture is important to merchants), goes to the stables, and cuts off the head of her husband's favorite horse with a saber. When she gives birth, she even cuts the head of her baby (cuts the head of the future). One could say that, psychologically, when women are treated poorly by society, charged to carry the archetypal shadow, and have the patriarchy battling them as matriarchal enemies, they are at risk of turning dangerously violent against men and women—and their selves. In fact, we see that her husband has intuited that his wife could "hurt herself or the baby." So, if he had some measure of intuition in his personality—as he demonstrates—we can ask why he took a sorceress as a wife, stayed with the evil figure, and "obeyed her orders?"

To help answer this question, one can recall experiences in clinical work. Commonly, men allow their wives to carry their anima—and don't develop their own. This means they do not believe in their feelings and do not work to develop their feeling function. They delegate that task to their wives. Some women are indeed delighted to control their husbands. Because arms represent the capacity to give and receive, one could say that these wives cut off the arms of their husband's feelings.

On the other hand, one could ponder that a part of the intial situation includes a negative mother complex. The brother is dealing with a destructive inner mother and—through the agency of his wife—acting out her orders against the other feminine figure—the sister. (Who, in a sense, he treats like a little mother, not a little sister: take care of this, take care of that.) Perhaps the situation with his negative mother already existed before the mother died or was generated by the unconscious of the brother himself. In any case, his wife became his dead mother.

One could ponder now for a moment the wife's violence: she uses a saber to cut off the horse's head. That's not a small task. She needs to be energetic to do that. It looks like a task for a strong man—or several strong men.

Perhaps a negative Animus coming from her own mother or father? A saber is masculine and phallic, like the sword, and the spear. It is an attribute of Mars. Not a primitive weapon like the club or ax, the saber—as well as the sword—presupposes metallurgical refinement, skilled artisans to make it, and elite training to practice its deadly art. Truly, the sorceress uses all her refinement to go against the heroine and even tries mockery at the very end, when she fears that her trickster side will be revealed. From this point of view, the tale appears to tell us that in the battle generated by giant complexes, women might react with instinctual, unconscious revenge, and refined war weapons. Which, of course, can be read about in the news, and, as psychotherapists, one can meet confined to prisons and mental hospitals. One could also list the ones who killed themselves or/and their children, as in this tale.

Now, one could pause for a moment before entering the Intensification phase and talk about the symbol of the horse, which the brother is proud to have in his stable. The horse is a god's mount, representing lightning, sun/moon rays, waves, and winds. It is also considered the mount of the Devil or witches—a phallus related to the broomstick. A solar animal, the horse is related to the wheel and the cosmos, connected with Helios, and pulls the sun-chariot by day. It is also seen as the body, with the spirit as the rider. In fact, working with this tale, one could have the opportunity to talk about the transformations brought about by the Spirit, and, a little later, one could talk about an illuminated new baby born in a manger, in the biblical stable.

The illuminated baby, a promise to the future (in contrast to the baby killed by the Great Mother-sorcerer), goes together with the stable. The stable symbolizes darkness, from which the sun emerges, or where the light-hero is born—like Jesus. It also represents light and revelation emerging from ignorance—which certainly happens in this individuation and redemption story.

Intensification: This is the way that leads to the turning point. It is often actually represented in fairy tales as a road that the hero has to travel. In some cases, various turning points can already be found within this intensification phase.

This story represents a road that the heroine has to travel, and several turning points will be found in this phase.

The reader is informed that, after the wife has convinced her husband that his sister has killed their baby, he "did not say anything; he wept bitter tears and turned away." Night came. At the stroke of midnight, he rose and said: "Little sister, make ready; we are going to Mass." She does not want to go; it is not a holiday that day, but still too early. "No, little sister, it is not early; it is high time to be gone," he tells her. Here is where the intensification starts. It is not early; it is high time for her to go to her sacrifice—to go to that Christmas midnight Mass, in which Christians get together to relive the suffering of Christ, but also to celebrate the promise of resurrection.

And there, in the woods, he cuts off her arms. Arms, as we know, are necessary to give and to receive. The little sister is left alone; she bursts into tears and begins to walk in the woods; she was all scratched but could not find a path out of the woods" (the unconscious situation.) Finally, after several years, she found a path.

This part of the story could remind us of Miles Davis, a famous American jazz trumpeter who said: "It takes a long time to learn how to play like yourself." An affirmation that the author is delighted to translate from the musical to the psychological realm: It takes a long time to find your own path to individuation.

A long time after wandering in her shadow, the sister, now *out of the woods*, came to a market town and stood beneath the window of the wealthiest merchant to beg for alms. In that house were a mother and a father—a new turning point in this intensification phase. And the father and mother loved their only son, who fell in love with the beggar woman and asked his parents to marry him to her. The story tells the reader that the son was their life's treasure—even though the merchant was the wealthiest one in town. So, they were reluctant to do what the son desired. But they got together with their community and modestly consulted God (in a new archetypal turning point.) "They gathered all the merchants and clerics and asked them to judge the matter: should they marry their son to the beggar woman or not?" The priest said: "Such must be his faith, and God gives your son his sanction to marry the beggar woman."

So, the community is involved in that important decision—as the Christian community comes together to the midnight Mass at Christmas.

The son lived with the girl for two years. The symbolic nature of number two represents symmetry, polarity, and discrimination, life experienced in duality, in polar tension, as the Chinese name it—yang and yin. C. G. Jung stated, "In dreams, we observe that motifs of two identical things have to do with (*border or liminal*) phenomena. These contents have just arrived at the border between consciousness and the unconscious."[20] Thus, number 2 is necessary for consciousness and relationships.

Then, the heroine's husband went to another province, where her brother had his shop. One could predict that the tale is now reuniting the different characters and their interiority, conflicts, development possibilities, and one dead-end road. As he leaves, the heroine's husband expresses the following feeling function message: "Dear father and mother, do not abandon my wife; as soon as she gives birth to a child, write to me that very hour." Which stands in opposition to what one has witnessed her brother do. One can interpret that the heroine's husband has healthy-feeling arms.

And here's the gift: Two or three months later (evolution from 2 to 3, representing the masculine energy), the girl gave birth to a child. The story describes the child to the reader: "His arms were golden up to the elbows, his sides were studded with stars, there was a bright moon on his forehead and a radiant sun near his heart. The grandparents were overjoyed and once wrote their beloved son a letter."

That letter, though, was intercepted by the hero's sorceress wife, who tricked the old man (who probably represents the old complex) into bringing the father a different message. She charmed him with talk and food—as witches do in some other stories—tore the original letter and substituted it for another which said: "Your wife has given birth to a half dog and half bear that she conceived with beasts in the woods." The messenger handed that false letter to the merchant's son, who read it and burst into tears. As we mentioned earlier, he consciously and warmly responded to his parents, asking that his son would not be molested until his return. He said: "When I come back, I will see what kind of baby it is."

As in the Devil's work, we observe in other stories that the brother's wife once more stole that letter and substituted it for a new one, ordering that the heroine should be driven out the moment they received the letter. The father and mother were grieved by the message and pondered that their son was causing them a lot of trouble: "We married him to the girl, and now he does not want his wife!" they concluded. So, the situation is getting more convoluted by the moment, and the false accusations –previously a part of the heroine's situation—are now extended to her husband by the very parents who were warm parental figures to her. They pitied not so much the wife, as the baby. So, they blessed her and the baby, tied it to her breast, and sent her away.

Here, the fairy tale moves into a new phase.

Turning Point: This can be recognized by the fact that another kind of behavior occurs after it. It is the moment in which the transformation being prepared by the intensification becomes manifest. The transformation proves itself real through a change in the action.

Here is the heroine, shedding bitter tears again. She walked for a long time, all in the open field, and no wood or village was anywhere. One could feel that she is abandoned again. But one can pause for a moment and consider that there are a lot of tears in this story—the heroine cries and her husband as well. Tears can be considered a sign of sorrow or ecstatic joy but can also indicate fertility. "The tears of the gods" are rain, the fertilizing Upper Waters, especially when they are "golden tears"–e.g., those of Demeter, Freya, and the tears of Isis: the fertilizing Nile. In Rapunzel's tale, as another example, one may recall that the prince is healed, recovering his sight when the heroine's tears touch his blind eyes. As we go along with the girl's story, there is a promise of fertility.

The story proceeds to tell the reader the heroine came to a dale and was very thirsty—does the word "dale" remind us of the Christian expression, "a valley of tears?" As she was thirsty, she looked to the right (the future) and saw a well. In fact, a well is seen as the feminine principle, the womb of the Great Mother; the psyche. Having contact with the underworld, the well often contains magic waters with healing powers. In Celtic mythology, sacred wells give access to the other world, have magical properties, and contain healing waters.

The heroine wanted to drink from that well but was afraid to bend over, lest she drop her baby. Then—marvelously!—she fancied that the water came closer. A hint that the Divine presence had her intentions in mind. So, she stooped to drink, and her baby fell into the well. She began to walk around the well, weeping and wondering how to get her child out of the well. An old man came to her and said: "Why are you weeping, you the *slave of God*?" She responded: How can I help not to weep? I stooped over the well to drink water, and my baby fell into it."

The man said: "Bend down and take him out." "No, little father, I cannot; I have no hands, only stumps." The man insisted: "Do as I tell you. Take your baby." She went to the well, stretched out her arms, and *God helped*, for suddenly she had her hands, all whole. She bent down, pulled her baby out, and began to give thanks to God, bowing to all four sides. One could interpret that the old man, in the story, represents an Angel or the Holy Spirit who recognizes her as a good slave of God, who had honored all shadows, all bad hands of cards she had received during her life, and was still trying to save her wonderful baby, that bridge to the future given to her by God.

So, the crucial point, the Turning Point in this story, occurs when *the heroine realizes that she has the power to rescue the child and save him from the waters of the unconscious.*

This scene also expresses a dramatic contrast to the action of the sister-in-law, who cuts off the head of her baby with a saber as soon as the child is born.

In any case, the reader can witness this remarkable fact in our life and the lives of others that an apparent disgrace (the girl dropping her baby in the well) leads to her miraculous healing, when she follows the voice of the Spirit in her, the voice of her Animus. *As she stretches her arms, now she has arms and hands and bows to the four directions* (the number four represents wholeness, totality, completion, solidarity, the Earth, and the four rivers of Paradise.) She is immensely grateful and says her prayers—now with hands and arms!—and advances in the path of her transformation.

In the beginning, she had been a little sister who would accept all her brother would determine for her to suffer, to the point of cutting off her arms without allowing her to say a word in her defense. Having not contradicted the false accusations slapped by her sister-in-law, our heroine marches decisively toward the house where her brother and husband are staying and asks for shelter. Not only has she already found shelter inside herself, and in the Spirit, but she will also now be her own person.

Again, we see the sorcerer trying to send her away, but new developments are happening, and the heroine's husband calls her brother *his* brother. One could certainly interpret that these two men are at different levels of development—very different fellows. Or is that recognition, in the story, that we all belong to the same family as humans? A hint of redemption, as the heroine marches toward them. Here, the brother (following his wife) and the girl's husband disagree on whether or not the beggar woman should stay. The heroine's husband is interested in hearing her because "beggar women can tell stories and recount real happenings," he says. Of course, they know well the "valley of tears" and developed their feeling function—and, in the case of this tale's heroine, her spiritual function and intuition; she has demonstrated her sensate side from the beginning. With help from her husband, they let her in. Her husband says: "Now, little dove, tell us a tale—any kind of story." He is considerate; he is warm.

Again, a dove represents the life spirit, the soul, the passing from one state or world to another, the spirit of light. Doves are sacred to all Great Mothers and Queens of Heaven and depict femininity and maternity. The dove with an olive branch is a symbol of peace, of renewal of life. And, of course, a traditional image of the Holy Spirit.

Now, the stage is ready for the heroine to tell a story. She is seated on the stove with her baby. That could remind the reader of the sacred fire of the furnace and the forge, with the power of alchemical transmutation of the flame; the generative, masculine, active, inflicting force in conjunction with the passive, receptive, enduring female crucible.

Then the heroine declares: "I do not know any tales or stories, but I can tell the truth." She recounts her own story from the beginning to that moment, in that place, including all the characters who are listening to her, with the ones who acted violently, immorally, and all. The sister-in-law tried numerous times to interrupt her, calling her names, and ordering her to stop. But her husband insisted that the girl continue, and turning to the brother said, in a masculine way: "Brother, order your wife to keep quiet; it is a wonderful story, is it not?" But as the evil woman continued to interrupt and the brother could not oppose her, the heroine's husband said again: "Brother, order her to keep quiet; why does she always interrupt?"

One could interpret all these interruptions as examples of what happens when unconscious complexes try incessantly to submerge one's conscious thoughts with criticism and the like. In fact, considering the tale *The Ill-fated Princess*, Verena Kast observes: "Refusing to back down until she has given her Moira what she must to receive the better fate that she has earned, (the heroine) refuses to accept the tyranny of self-destructive thoughts. And she shows her intrapsychic persistence. The girl's persistence in showing her nurturing side drives the specter away."[21]

In this tale, as the heroine came to the point in the story when she was let in and began to tell the truth instead of a story, she pointed at the people who were listening to her and *confronted* them. She said: "This is my husband, this is my brother, and this is my sister-in-law."

Concluding Situation: An entirely new situation emerges due to the transformation.

The new situation is that the heroine's husband "jumped up to her on the stove and said: 'Now, my dear, show me the baby. Let me see whether my father and mother wrote me the truth.' They took the baby, removed its swaddling clothes, and illuminated the whole room! 'So, it is true,' he exclaimed, 'that she did not tell us just a tale; here is my wife, and here is my son—golden up to the elbows, his sides studded with stars, a bright moon on his forehead, and a radiant sun near his heart!' With that, he also confronted the evil woman and the evil brother, affirming his truth as his wife had done. A strong redemption is now present. The young husband sees the Divine Presence in his son, whom he is seeing for the first time—with golden arms to embrace his feelings, studded with stars reflecting the beauty of God, a bright moon from Mother Earth to clarify his inner world, and a radiant masculine sun near a generous heart.

As a result of this clarification, the ex-sheep brother "took his best mare from his stable, tied the sorceress wife to his tail, and let it run *in the open field*. The mare dragged her to the ground until she brought back only her braid; the rest was strewn on the field. One could find interesting the correspondence the tale appears to establish between the fact that the mare dragged the wicked woman on the ground in the open field and that same expression was used at the beginning of what we saw as the turning point phase. There, the heroine, shedding bitter tears, walked all over the open field for a long time, and there was no wood or village anywhere. What a contrasting scene! Both are scenes of purgation.

Verena Kast points out, "In many fairy tales, the witch is burned. She must always be combated and overcome for the action to proceed further in a living way. That is the archetypal requirement of the human maturation process."[22]

On the other hand, this is also a story about the development of the brother's anima, who, in the end, through suffering, begins to become conscious of herself.

The last piece of information one is given in *The Armless Maiden* is that the remaining characters harnessed three horses (the number three being a primarily masculine number, as well as the horses) and went home to the young husband's father and mother, where they began living happily and prospered.

The tale, thus, brings about a happy ending, in a story of individuation and spiritual redemption, with the number 4 (the heroine and husband, baby, and brother) saying thanks to God, bowing to all four directions.

INTERPRETATION OF HANS: THE HEDGEHOG

The Type

Checking "The Types of the Folktale, a Classification, and Bibliography," by Anti Aarne and the following authors (1981 version,) the type of this Fairy Tale is number 441, listed as *Hans My Hedgehog.* In that Fairy Tale, in summary, a childless woman gives birth to a hedgehog. Two kings unwittingly promise the hedgehog their daughter when the latter shows each of them the way out of the forest. One of the kings promises his daughter and attempts to evade the promise. The other king and his daughter are faithful to the promise. Hedgehog takes the bride; the hero's skin is burned; he is disenchanted and changes into a handsome youth.[23]

One can associate *Hans My Hedgehog* to the more general category 425, *The Monster as Husband*: the monster is born because of the inconsiderate wish of parents (in this case, the father), and, in the end, the hero is disenchanted by destroying his skin. Other tales which can be associated with *Hans My Hedgehog* are *Cupid and Psyche* (425A), *Beauty and the Beast* (425C), and *Bird Husband* (425N), among others.

The type of fairy tle expressed in *Hans My Hedgehog*, or variations of it, can be found in the following cultures: Estonian, Lithuanian, Swedish, Norwegian, Flemish, German, Hungarian, Czech, Slovenian, Serbo-Croatian, Polish, and Russian.

One could examine the development of this fairy tale following four phases, as suggested by Verena Kast in "Witches, Ogres, and the Devil's Daughter": the initial situation, intensification, turning point, and concluding situation.

Hans: The Hedgehog

There was once a countryman who had money and land in plenty, but no matter how rich he was, one thing was still wanting in his happiness: he had no children. Often when he went into the town with the other peasants, they mocked him and asked why he had no children. At last, he became angry, and when he got home, he said, "I will have a child, even if it is a hedgehog."

Then his wife had a child, that was a hedgehog in the upper part of his body and a boy in the lower. When she saw the child, she was terrified, and said, "See, there thou hast brought ill-luck on us." Then said the man, "What can be done now? The boy must be christened, but we shall not be able to get a godfather for him." The woman said, "And we cannot call him anything else but 'Hans the Hedgehog.'"

When he was christened, the parson said, "He cannot go into any ordinary bed because of his spikes." So, a little straw was put behind the stove, and Hans the Hedgehog was laid on it. His mother could not suckle him, for he would have pricked her with his quills. So, he lay there behind the stove for eight years, and his father was tired of him and thought, "If he would but die!"

He did not die, however, but remained lying there. Now it happened that there was a fair in the town, and the peasant was about to go to it and asked his wife what he should bring back with him for her. "A little meat and a couple of white rolls, which are wanted for the house," said she. Then he asked the servant, and she wanted a pair of slippers and some stockings with clocks.

At last, he said also, "And what wilt thou have, Hans, my Hedgehog?" "Dear father," he said, "do bring me bagpipes." When, therefore, the father came home again, he gave his wife what he had bought for her; meat and white rolls, and then he gave the maid the slippers and the stockings with clocks; and, lastly, he went behind the stove, and gave Hans the Hedgehog the bagpipes.

And when Hans the Hedgehog had the bagpipes, he said, "Dear father, do go to the forge and get the cock shod, and then I will ride away, and never come back again." On this, the father was delighted to think that he was going to get rid of him and had the cock shod for him, and when it was done, Hans the Hedgehog got on it and rode away, but took swine and asses with him, which he intended to keep in the forest.

When they got there, he made the cock fly onto a high tree with him, and there he sat for many a long year and watched his asses and swine until the herd was quite large, and his father knew nothing about him. While sitting in the tree, however, he played his bagpipes and made very beautiful music.

Once, a king came traveling by who had lost his way and heard the music. He was astonished at it and sent his servant forth to look all around and see from whence this music came. He spied about but saw nothing but a little animal sitting up aloft on the tree, which looked like a cock with a hedgehog on it which made this music.

Then the king told the servant he was to ask why he sat there, and if he knew the road which led to his kingdom. So, Hans the Hedgehog descended from the tree and said he would show the way if the king would write a bond and promise him whatever he first met in the royal courtyard as soon as he arrived home. Then the king thought, "I can easily do that, Hans the Hedgehog understands nothing, and I can write what I like."

So, the king took pen and ink and wrote something, and when he had done it, Hans the Hedgehog showed him the way, and he got safely home. But the king's daughter, when she saw him from afar, was so overjoyed that she ran to meet him, and kissed him. Then he remembered Hans the Hedgehog and told her what had happened, and that he had been forced to promise whatsoever first met him when he got home, to a very strange animal which sat on a cock as if it were a horse and made beautiful music, but that instead of writing that he should have what he wanted, he had written that he should not have it. The princess was glad and said he had done well, for she would never have gone away with the Hedgehog.

Hans the Hedgehog, however, looked after his asses and pigs, and was always merry and sat on the tree and played his bagpipes.

Now it came to pass that another king came journeying by with his attendants and runners, and he also had lost his way and did not know how to get home again because the forest was so large. He likewise heard the beautiful music from a distance and asked his runner what that could be and told him to go and see.

Then the runner went under the tree and saw the cock sitting at the top of it, and Hans the Hedgehog on the cock. The runner asked him what he was about up there. "I am keeping my asses and my pigs; but what is your desire?" The messenger said that they had lost their way, and could not get back into their own kingdom, and asked if he would not show them the way. Then Hans the Hedgehog got down the tree with the cock and told the aged king that he would show him the way, if he would give him for his own whatsoever first, met him in front of his royal palace.

The king said, "Yes," and wrote a promise to Hans the Hedgehog that he should have this. That done, Hans rode on before him on the cock, and pointed out the way, and the king reached his kingdom again in safety. When he got to the courtyard, there were great rejoicings.

Now he had an only daughter who was very beautiful; she ran to meet him, threw her arms around his neck, and was delighted to have her old father back again. She asked him where in the world he had been for so long. So he told her how he had lost his way, and had very nearly not come back at all, but that as he was traveling through a great forest, a creature, half hedgehog, half man, who was sitting astride a cock in a high tree, and making music, had shown him the way and helped him to get out, but that in return he had promised him whatsoever first met him in the royal courtyard, and how that was she herself, which made him unhappy now. But on this, she promised that, for the love of her father, she would willingly go with this Hans if he came.

Hans the Hedgehog, however, took care of his pigs, and the pigs multiplied until they became so many in number that the whole forest was filled with them.

Then Hans the Hedgehog resolved not to live in the forest any longer and sent word to his father to have every sty in the village emptied, for he was coming with such a great herd that all might kill who wished to do so. He was troubled when his father heard that, for he thought Hans the Hedgehog had died long ago. Hans the Hedgehog, however, seated himself on the cock, drove the pigs before him into the village, and ordered the slaughter to begin. Ha! But a killing and a chopping might have been heard two miles off!

After this Hans the Hedgehog said, "Father, let me have the cock shod once more at the forge, and then I will ride away and never come back as long as I live." Then the father had the cock shod once more and was pleased that Hans the Hedgehog would never return again.

Hans the Hedgehog rode away to the first kingdom. There the king had commanded that whosoever came mounted on a cock and had bagpipes with him should be shot at, cut down, or stabbed by everyone so that he might not enter the palace. When, therefore, Hans the Hedgehog came riding thither, they all pressed forward against him with their pikes, but he spurred the cock, and it flew up over the gate in front of the king's window and lighted there, and Hans cried that the king must give him what he had promised, or he would take both his life and his daughter's.

Then the king began to speak to his daughter fairly and beg her to go away with Hans to save her own life and her father's. So, she dressed in white, and her father gave her a carriage with six horses and magnificent attendants, together with gold and possessions. She seated herself in the carriage and placed Hans the Hedgehog beside her with the cock and the bagpipes, and then they took leave and drove away, and the king thought he should never see her again.

He was, however, deceived in his expectation, for when they were at a short distance from the town, Hans the Hedgehog took her pretty clothes off and pierced her with his hedgehog's skin until she bled all over. "That is the reward of your falseness," said he, "go your way, I will not have you!" and on that, he chased her home again, and she was disgraced for the rest of her life.

Hans the Hedgehog, however, rode on further on the cock, with his bagpipes, to the dominions of the second king to whom he had shown the way. This one, however, had arranged that if anyone resembling Hans the Hedgehog should come, they were to present arms, give him safe conduct, cry long life to him, and lead him to the royal palace. But when the king's daughter saw him, she was terrified, for he looked quite too strange. She remembered, however, that she could not change her mind, for she had given her promise to her father. So, Hans the Hedgehog was welcomed by her, married to her, and had to go with her to the royal table. She seated herself by his side, and they ate and drank.

When the evening came and they wanted to go to sleep, she was afraid of his quills, but he told her she was not to fear, for no harm would befall her, and he told the old king that he was to appoint four men to watch by the door of the chamber, and light a great fire, and when he entered the room and was about to get into bed, he would creep out of his hedgehog's skin and leave it lying there by the bedside, and that the men were to run nimbly to it, throw it in the fire, and stay by it until it was consumed.

When the clock struck eleven, he went into the chamber, stripped off the hedgehog's skin, and left it lying by the bed. Then came the men and fetched it swiftly and threw it in the fire; and when the fire had consumed it, he was delivered, and lay there in bed in human form, but he was coal-black as if he had been burnt. The King sent for his physician, who washed him with precious salves and anointed him, and he became white and was a handsome young man. When the King's daughter saw that, she was glad, and the next morning, they arose joyfully, ate, and drank, and then the marriage was properly solemnized, and Hans the Hedgehog received the kingdom from the aged king.

When several years passed, he went with his wife to his father and said he was his son. The father, however, declared he had no son; he had never had but one, and he had been born like a hedgehog with spikes and had gone forth into the world. Then Hans made himself known, and the old father rejoiced and went with him to his kingdom.

> My tale is done,
> And away it has run . . .

These words are expected at the end of Russian fairy tales and traditional stories in that region, like the shadow signature of the person telling what has happened, a type of "The End."

Initial situation: This is the existing condition that brings about the story, to begin with.

What one could first learn is that Hedgehog's father "*had money and land in plenty*"—so, there was no problem in terms of the family's economic situation. The problem was that he had no children, and this one thing "*was still wanting in his happiness*." Moreover, that initial situation, which is an image of the problem at hand that the fairy tale is going to work with, was aggravated by the mocking of the other peasants asking why he had no children. One could interpret that this community is a very patriarchal one (more about that in a minute), where men are expected to generate children to prove their manhood. The father of our hero was appearing in front of his peers, the ones who could validate him, as having a problem of infertility in his own house. So much so that, "*at last he became angry, and when he got home, he said, 'I will have a child, even if it be a hedgehog.'*"

That initial situation gets increasingly problematic for, after the countryman announcement, his wife had a child who "*was a hedgehog in the upper part of his body, and a boy in the lower, and when she saw the child, she was terrified.* She said, "*See, there thou hast brought ill luck on us.*" Now the man was again accused, this time in his own house. Then, when the child was christened, the parson noted that the hedgehog could not "*go into any ordinary bed because of his spikes*"—which can hint at the father's bed and the father's "spikes" in his own relationship with his wife.

We are then told that a little straw was put behind the stove, and Hans the Hedgehog was laid on it. His mother could not suckle him, for he would have pricked her with his quills (which, of course, constitutes another rupture—a serious problem in the mother-child relationship). We can see that the mother is there, who provides a little feminine warmth (the stove in the kitchen) but does not seem to be a good enough presence. And we are informed that our hero "*lay behind the stove for eight years, and his father was tired of him and thought, "If he would but die!"*"

So, the hero is rejected by both parents, who are ashamed of him. There is almost no space for him in their house and their life, and his father "wishes" for his death.

One could think for a moment about these problems in the tale's initial situation, which will bring about the story. First of all, we can find the same father's inconsiderate wish in other parents in other fairy tales, like in "The Raven," for example (where the mother says to her baby daughter: "I wish you were a raven") and "the wish" becomes true. Here, the "wish" occurs even before the child is born—meaning that, if we take the story to express the suffering of a real child, we are looking at very early trauma, it will take a long time to be treated.

On the other hand, the failure to have a child in the tale can be seen as a physical event. Still, one could interpret as it can also show us an image of a psychological inadequacy in the couple's relationship—the couple cannot produce a child, the symbol of joyful creativity, the bridge to the future. So, there is helplessness here, and the shadow in the personality of the bullied father, his dramatic anger for not having things his way, (in other words, his unconscious complexes, his superego) are constellated.

One can see, as the tale unfolds, that, in a sense, the thinking type father's shadow (he will "show them" that he is capable of having a child!) and his rage is inherited by the son. This situation will generate Hedgehog's heroic quest to survive his father's curse (we can think of a hedgehog rolling upon himself in self-defense to protect his vulnerable flesh), and deal with his own shadow.

In fact, in Christian terms, the hedgehog is associated with the Evil One and to evil doing—rob vines of grapes as the Devil robs men of souls. Other symbols for a hog list are filth, impurity, voracity, and sensuality—Circe changed Odysseus' companions into hogs. The hedgehog is also associated with demonic possession, seen as a frequent companion of witches, and is believed to be a weather prognosticator: when it comes out of hibernation, if it sees its own *shadow,* it retires into its burrow, and winter will last for six more weeks.

The inner reality is that the child is abandoned by his shadow and will be a shadow character for much of his evolution until he is redeemed.

One could conclude these thoughts about the tale's initial situation by asking the following question: what can we make of the fact that the child "was a hedgehog in the upper part of his body and a boy in the lower"? Apparently, the community that generated the story was a very primitive one. The people described in the story are still strongly immersed in a life of instinctual impulses—they behave as half-humans. As the ruptured image of the hedgehog appears to suggest, they behave as a half-human, half-animal. They are still unconscious in a significant part of their personality and still struggling to become conscious.

Intensification: This is the way that leads to the turning point. It is often represented in fairy tales as a road the hero has to travel. In some cases, various turning points can already be found within this intensification phase.

The intensification phase leads to the turning point. In this story, it is actually represented as a road that the hero has to travel, and several turning points will be found in this intensification phase.

The reader is informed that Hedgehog did not die as a result of the second inconsiderate "wish" of his father, and remained lying on the little carpet until there was a fair in the town. A fair can remind us of many people and contents brought together, as a renewal or reorganization of inner reality. Hedgehog is now eight years old. In traditional symbols, eight represents spirituality, and the goal of the initiate after having passed through the seven stages or heavens, and it is, thus, the number of Paradise regained regeneration and resurrection. In Christian symbolism, the eighth day created the new man of grace. After seven days of fasting and penance, the eight days become full of renewal.

The peasant, then, goes to the fair, brings back to his wife "a little meat and a couple of white rolls she had asked for the house," and to the servant, "a pair of slippers and some stockings with clocks" she wanted. These requests appear to represent the interest and role of the lady of the house (to bring food from the outside world) and the servant's interest to be seen as attractive.

Given that we now see a pair of slippers and stockings with clocks, one can probably hint that "the clock is ticking" in an intensified mode.

In fact, after the father goes behind the stove and gives Hedgehog the bagpipes he wanted from the fair, the son asks the father to go to the forge, get the cock shod, and then he will ride away and never come back again. The father is delighted at the news and brings the cock shod, Hans the Hedgehog gets on it and rides away, but takes swine and asses with him, which he intended to keep in the forest.

So, here is Hans the Hedgehog mounted on a cock and on the road to the forest, a symbol of the unconscious. Arriving there, we are told, "he made the cock fly onto a high tree with him, and there he sat for many a long year and watched his asses and swine until the herd was quite large, and his father knew nothing about him." While sitting in the tree, however, he played his bagpipes and made beautiful music. This side of Hedgehog is interesting because music, especially beautiful music, can be considered to represent the harmony of the universe on the outside, and life harmony, in the inner world. That tree can also be associated with the Tree of Life of his own story.

One could also look at the animals which are connected to him. First, the cock, which he is mounting, even on the top of the high tree. The cock is a solar bird, associated with the masculine principle (the word "cock" frequently denotes the penis), and symbolizes supremacy, courage, vigilance, and the dawn. Our hero establishes himself at the top of the high tree with his cock, reminding us of the many Protestant churches in Germany which display the figure of a cock at their steeple (the cock greets the dawn of the sun of Christ.)

That cock, by the way, was given to him by his father—another inheritance—as well as the asses and the swine. The asses represent humility and obstinacy but also potent fertility. They also typified the flight into Egypt and the triumphal entry into Jerusalem. The pigs are also a fertility symbol, hence prosperity, but also gluttony, greed, lust, anger, and unbridled passion. In many ancient cultures, the swine symbolized the heavily fecund—but possibly devouring—Great Mother. One could interpret that all his animals could bring us into the road of recognizing them as a type of compensation or counterbalancing of infertility in his parent's relationship, which caused Hedgehog so much suffering.

The fact that, in spite of his trauma, our hero was able to play beautiful music with his bagpipes at the top of the tree appears to suggest that he had a preserved side of intuition and spirituality in his personality. Music instruments denote felicity. The image of the bagpipes can also be seen as a form of "hedgehog" with their protruding "spikes." Like other pipe instruments, they are phallic compared to many stringed instruments representing the female form.

One could also observe the other turning points presented in this intensification phase. Two kings, first one then the other, who had lost their way to return home, hear the beautiful music, and meet Hedgehog in the forest. They both ask for his advice to find their way to return to their castle. Their common problem, of course, means that both kings have lost their conscious way of orientation and are now immersed in the unconscious (the forest). They both seek help from the astonishing half-hedgehog, half man who lives in the forest, plays beautiful music, and is positioned at a much higher level than the authority of these lost kings. He is mounting a cock like a sun and sees everything around from the top of a tall tree. So, both kings ask him for directions.

At that, Hedgehog *descended from his tree*—a gesture of a generous royal person!—to the level of each lost king, who said he would be willing to help them, but at a price: each must sign a bond promising the hero "whatever he first met in the royal courtyard as soon as he arrived home." We can recall that his request is common in fairy tales.

Here, the two visiting lost kings display a different performance, later causing significantly different results for them and their families. The different value choices made by each king—another turning point—show us the different levels of their inner development and consciousness. It shows us, also, the sequence of Hedgehog's own psychological development described by the tale, as he first meets the king who acts like a violent trickster and, later on, the wise old king.

The first king, a rational type, could remind the reader of the hero's primitive, authoritarian father, who started this story with his inconsiderate wish. This first visiting king believes he knows everything, unlike the strange Hedgehog. When asked to sign a bond to obtain the needed directions, the king thinks: *"I can easily do that. Hans the Hedgehog understands nothing, and I can write what I like."* So, *he took pen and ink and wrote something, and when he had done it, Hans the Hedgehog showed him the way, and he got safely home.* So, the king apparently agrees with Hedgehog's request but has no intention of honoring his promise—certainly a shadow action.

That shadow displayed by the first king resonates also in his daughter's character, for when he tells her that *he had been forced to promise whatever first met him when he got home and that instead of writing that he should have what he wanted, he had written that he should not have it,* the princess was glad. *She proclaimed that her father had done well, for she would never have gone away with the Hedgehog.*

Her reply, of course, could remind one of the hero's own mother's disgusted, rejecting, ashamed reaction when the hero was born. In fact, his mother had not been able to *suckle him, for he would have pricked her with his quills.* That serious initial rupture with the feminine figure (the negative

Great Mother) will be again presented when we see this king's daughter in a very different situation for a second time.

For now, we are told that *Hans the Hedgehog looked after his asses and pigs and was always merry and sat on the tree and played with his bagpipes.*

A little later, here comes a second king—this one an aged king—who *also had lost his conscious way and did not know how to get home again.* He, likewise, entered the unconscious level (*"the forest was so large!")* and heard the beautiful music which fascinated these kings. Truly, this is a different fascination than the one produced by their authority and power over their community. In fact, Hedgehog is placed higher than the king's level; they must look up to him for directions—like he was some god.

In this encounter, one is told that the king's runner asks Hedgehog *what he was about up there.* And the hero responds: *"I am keeping my asses and my pigs, but what is your desire?"* One could interpret this as another turning point already in the intensification phase. Now, for the first time, we hear the word "desire!"

So, Hedgehog, *in response to their "desire," tells the aged king that he would show him the way if he would give him for his own whatsoever first, met him in front of his royal palace.* This second king said *"Yes,"* but, in contrast to the first, *wrote a promise to Hans the Hedgehog that he should have this. That done, Hans rode on before him on the cock and pointed out the way, and the king reached his kingdom again in safety.*

The scene in the aged king's courtyard, though, was quite different from the one when the first king returned home. This second king had an only daughter who was very beautiful; she ran to meet him, threw her arms around his neck, and was delighted to have her old father back again.

She asked him where in the world he had been for so long. So, he told her he had lost his way and had nearly not returned. He was traveling through a great forest, though, and a creature, half hedgehog, half man, who was sitting astride a cock in a high tree, making music, had shown him the way and helped him to get out. But that in return, he had promised him whatsoever first met him in the royal courtyard, and how that was she herself, which made him unhappy now. But on this, she promised that, for the love of her father, she would willingly go with Hans if he came. A position, together with the one taken by her father, suggests that their feeling function was preserved.

With that, the reader is informed that the hero *took care of his pigs, and the pigs multiplied until they became so many in number that the whole forest was filled with them, possibly meaning* fertility is all over the place. Here, we proceed into a new phase.

Turning Point: This can be recognized because another behavior occurs afterward. It is the moment in which the transformation being prepared by the intensification becomes manifest. The transformation proves itself real through a change in the action.

The first step into this Turning Point phase is that Hans *the Hedgehog resolved not to live in the forest any longer.* One could interpret that as a sign that he is maturing as a human being; he decides to leave the unconscious mode and grow into a more conscious life. He *sends word to his father to have every stay in the village emptied, for he is coming with such a great herd that "all might kill who wished to do so."*

The father, who thought that Hans the Hedgehog had died long ago, was troubled. We know this situation from therapy. In fact, if a client gets healthier, there is a possibility that the family members will have to accommodate themselves to new roles! Someone else in that group might be unconsciously pushed into the psychological "emergent" position, which has been vacated by the person who gets better. The emergent member symbolically represents the "family problem," which occurs when, for defensive reasons, a group prefers to believe that "we would be so completely happy if only such and such was not that crazy." In that case, a possible change in the equilibrium feels scary.

So, we see Hans the Hedgehog, seated on the cock, drive the pigs before him into the village and order the slaughter to begin. "*Ha! But there was a killing and a chopping that might have been heard two miles off!*" says the text. One could consider that this great carnage represents the birth of the ego, which starts to battle against the new "organization" intended by the Self. Many of the hero's unconscious instincts (the hogs) are then brutally killed. That's what happens when the ego is born out of suffering. It is like Hedgehog deciding that many of his instincts will no longer rule (like his father's instinctual actions.)

After the carnage, Hans the Hedgehog declared, "*Father, let me have the cock shod once more at the forge, and then I will ride away and never come back as long as I live.*" Then the father had the cock shod once more and was pleased that Hans the Hedgehog would never return.

In fact, one could interpret that the father does not want to acknowledge an ugly part of himself and wants his own shadow—projected onto his son—to go away forever.

On the other hand, one could ponder that the theme of this tale is expressed in everyday life across different cultures in the world. If an athletic father, for example, wishes his son to be successful as a sports champion (perhaps a father's own dream) and the youth is more introverted and does not want—or can—realize the father's desire, that child will suffer greatly. Sometimes, sons and daughters are traumatized by their parents who have specific "plans" for them, remain blocked in their super egoic phantasy, and can only see what the child is not!

In the tale we are examining, our hero has demonstrated to his father the fertility and power of his herds and his own power in handling his effort successfully.

After that turning point, Hans the Hedgehog rode away to the first kingdom. There, the trickster king "*had commanded that whosoever came mounted on a cock and had bagpipes with him should be shot at, cut down, or stabbed by everyone so that he might not enter the palace. When, therefore, Hans the Hedgehog came riding thither, they all pressed forward against him with their pikes.*" The hero, though, "*spurred the cock. It flew up over the gate in front of the king's window and lighted there*"—an action that we can associate with the unconscious, which comes in even when people do not welcome it. In the king's palace, *Hans cried that* "*the king must give him what he had promised, or he would take both his life and his daughter's.*"

Then, the unconscious king implored his daughter to go away with Hans to save her own life and her father's. She was dressed in white, and her father gave her a carriage with six horses, magnificent attendants, gold, and possessions. With this new turning point, the king's daughter seated herself in the carriage, placed Hans the Hedgehog beside her with the cock and the bagpipes, and then they took leave and drove away.

In reproduction of what the Hedgehog's father twice believed, the king thought he should never see his daughter again. But, like Hans's father, he was deceived in his expectation. "*When they were at a short distance from the town, Hans the Hedgehog took her pretty clothes off and pierced her with his hedgehog's skin until she bled all over. 'That is the reward for your falseness,' said he. 'Go your way, I will not have you!' he chased her home again, and she was disgraced for the rest of her life.*"

One could certainly note that, like Hans's negative mother, who did not suckle him because of his spikes, the proud king's daughter really met the hero's spikes—in a worse way.

Concluding Situation: An entirely new situation emerges due to this transformation.

Having shown the trickster king and his daughter *the reward of* "*their falseness,*" Hans the Hedgehog rode on further on the cock, with his bagpipes, to the dominions of the second King to whom he had shown the way. This one, however, had arranged that if anyone resembling Hans, the Hedgehog should come, they would present arms, give him safe conduct, cry long life to him, and lead him to the royal palace.

When she saw him, the king's daughter was also terrified, but probably on a different level of consciousness, she remembered her promise to her father. So, Hans, the Hedgehog, was welcomed by her and married her.

The tale tells us that "When the evening came, and they wanted to sleep, she was afraid of his quills." Hans told her, though, that she was not to fear, for no harm would befall her, and he told the old king that he was to appoint four men to watch by the door of the chamber and light a great fire. When he entered the room and was about to get into bed, he would creep out of his hedgehog's skin and leave it lying there by the bedside, and the men were to run nimbly to it, throw it in the fire, and stay by it until it was consumed."

At this point, we will witness the power of fire in the hero's redemption. Fire is a symbol of transformation and purification. It represents the generative power of the sun—like the cock waiting for the dawn at the church's steeple and the bird mounted by the hero. Fire symbolizes the renewal of life, impregnation, power, strength, energy, the unseen energy in existence, sexual power, passion, and also a passage from one state to another, which is the point where we are here.

When the clock struck eleven (meaning the presence of peril—ten being the perfect number and the law, eleven representing the exceeding of both), the hero went into the chamber, "stripped off the hedgehog's skin, and left it lying by the bed. Then came the men and fetched it swiftly and threw it in the fire; and when the fire had consumed it, he was delivered, and lay there in bed in human form, but he was coal black as if he had been burnt." One could interpret his coal black aspect as the expression of the shadow, which had been with him. He is shown burned and as black as coal because of his suffering. In fact, fire is very painful, and he had been in the fire all his life. The burnt is the mark of that fire. One is reminded of his wounds.

But here also, there is powerful redemption: the good father figure, the aged king, "sent for his physician who washed" the hero "with precious salves, and anointed him, and he became white and was a handsome young man." He was healed from the scars of his suffering, from his burns.

When the king's daughter saw that, she was glad, and the next morning they arose joyfully, ate, and drank, and then the marriage was properly solemnized, and Hans the Hedgehog received the kingdom from the aged king.

There is still an extra redemption in *Hans, the Hedgehog* tale: the redemption of his inner father. One could note that his mother, like the trickster king's daughter, is not shown anymore. Anyways, the reader is told that, several years later, the hero "went with his wife to his father and said that he was his son. The father, however, declared *he had no son*; he had never had but one, and he had been born like a hedgehog with spikes and had gone forth into the world." Again, we see that the father pushes away the relationship with his son. He had wished his son to be dead several times previously and believed he was dead. Which the son really was, for him. Because he had no value in his father's eyes.

The fairy tale tells us that "Hans made himself known, and the old father rejoiced and went with him to his kingdom." One can still ponder that now, when the hero demonstrates he is a successful and considerate king—meaning an apparently more honorable extension of the father into the future—the father welcomes him. Even if that father has perhaps matured a little and is now a more conscious human being, he could not redeem himself. The son does that.

THE CERTIFICATE: A FINNISH FAIRY TALE

The Type

Checking "The Types of the Folktale, a Classification, and Bibliography," by Anti Aarne and the following authors, the type of this fairy tale appears to be number 465C, called *A Journey to the Other World.* In that type of fairy tale, a man receives his wife from God. A king (in this case, an emperor) sends him on a quest to the other world (to bring God from heaven, etc.)[24] The man succeeds with the help of his wife. The tale can also be included in the more general category 465, *The Man Persecuted Because of His Beautiful Wife.* In this more general group, the hero receives his wife from God, and the envious king who covets the wife gives the hero impossible tasks to accomplish. He must find the unknown food, the living harp, God in the other world, the wonderful flower, to bring tiger's milk to cure feigned sickness, to reap a field of grain (or the like) in one night or other tasks. He accomplishes these with the help of his wife. The king (in our particular tale, the emperor) is overcome and is punished (gets blind) as the advisor to the king in this more general type gets a punishment. One could also associate The Certificate with the general type 460A, *The Journey to God to Receive Reward,* where the hero meets God and receives his reward along with the answers to questions others have asked him in his journey.

We can find this type of Fairy Tale expressed in The Certificate, or variations of it, in the following cultures: Finnish, Livonian, Lithuanian, Russian, Ukrainian, and Turkish.

A young man had to care for his old blind parents and nourish them. That's why he couldn't marry the woman he wanted. One day he felt tired and thought: "Oh if I had a wife now who could cook me soup!" Soon afterward, he met an old man who asked him: "On what are you thinking?" He responded: "I have a blind father and a blind mother who can't cook a meal." "Well," said the old man, "at least I give you this stick." The young man took it but didn't think about it until he got hungry. He started looking at it—and behold! A girl stood at the roadside. He asked: "And who are you?" She answered: "I am your wife!" "Now let's go to the marriage!" he said. "No," responded the girl, "I don't go to the marriage, bring me first to your father and mother. Only then we go to the marriage."

They went to the mother and father and stayed together. Then they got a farm with servants and all the necessary things. The woman gave all the beggars the same help. The beggars also went to the emperor to get alms ("mild Gaben") from him. The emperor asked them: "What do you see in that house? Is it better than mine?" They responded: "We don't know. There's only a pretty woman we have never seen before. She is a very beautiful lady." The emperor started looking for her.

The man and his wife welcomed him politely, giving him food, drinks, and gifts. The emperor asked: "From where did you get this wife? Did you get her spontaneously or steal her from an emperor or someone else? Did you get her with violence?"

"I didn't take her with violence; God has given her to me."

"Well, why didn't God give me such a good wife as he gave to you? Go and bring to me within five days a certificate from God that he has given her to you and that you didn't steal her. Otherwise, I'll take away your wife."

The man was in great distress, but his wife said: "Don't fear anything! Go, I send you." She gave him her silk scarf and said: "Cross yourself on the road, then the way you have to go opens up."

In the evening, he asked two men in a house for a place for the night. They said: "It's cold here. We can't warm up the room. But you can stay overnight." The man wondered about that since he felt the room was too warm. In the morning, they asked him where he was going. As he said: "I'm seeking God, but I don't know where to find him." They bid him: "When you come to God, please ask him why we can't warm up our room."

The next evening, he came to a cottage where two women scooped water out of a ditch that went through the room. As he asked them, they allowed him to stay overnight. As he drank from the water, it was milk; he wondered why they said it was water. The next morning, learning that he was searching for God, they bid him: "Please ask God why we must scoop water in the last six years which never end in the ditch."

On the third evening, he asked an old woman whether he could stay overnight in her pretty cottage. She agreed with that but said: "I can't give you anything to eat, I must chew stones day and night." He gave her his bread, which became stone in her hands. The next morning, as he told her about his search for God, she bid him: "Please ask God why I must chew stones for the last twelve years,"

He continued walking and found a beautiful manor built of white stones. There he found God, who gave him the certificate attesting that God had given him his wife.

And God responded to the other questions: "The old woman must chew stones because of her richness with which she didn't help anybody who came to ask for it." "Which way can she get rid of her punishment?" asked the man.

"She will be free when I let come a big coldness so that the stars fall from the sky. If she can tolerate the cold, she can be free."

And why must two women endlessly scoop water which was fresh milk as I drank it?" the man asked. "They poured water into the milk they sold," God said. "Can they count on your grace if they got insight in their injustice?" "They will be free if they will be able to count the hairs of their cows in the big coldness I'll send," God responded.

"And why did two men live in the coldness while the room was warm as I came to them?" the man asked. "They didn't help any beggar, not even in the biggest coldness," God responded. "How can they get redeemed?" "When I send a horrible coldness, they can stand and can add together the stars of the sky, then I let them free," said God.

The man returned home with his certificate. The emperor came as a guest and took the headsman with him to immediately take the woman home. The emperor read the certificate and became blind right away. Then he said to the man: "Forgive me that I tormented you and your wife and let me go so that I don't get totally blind. Keep your wife and all your goods. Also, if I get back my eyesight, I will never again desire or touch your wife." The man showed mercy and forgave the emperor saying: "I forgive you, everything shall be forgiven and forgotten." Now the emperor got back his eyesight again. "Be my guest; I'll take care of you and never harass or touch you." Then they called each other cousins.

Soon afterward, God visited the man and the woman for a feast and dinner, saying: "Get up, I bring you the marriage."—"We come," said the woman. But then a coffin was carried to the yard. The blind parents of the man had died. God had taken their souls to him and ordered to bury them in the earth. God himself sang the funeral [fiú..] songs.

God then told them to visit the emperor who gave them a meal and drinks. The emperor said: "Forgive me, God, since I harassed the man."— "Well," said God, "I forgive you because the man has forgiven you."

Then they went to the men in the cold room. They invited God and the man to a meal, and they asked God: "Forgive us the wrong we had done in earlier times." God forgave them saying: "Live as you like but receive people who come and don't let them freeze."

Then they went to the women who served milk to God without water. "Don't ever pour water into the milk," said God and added: "I surely had delivered you to the fire of hell if the man hadn't come to me."

Then they went to the old woman. She brought them baked goods and asked God: "Please free me from the chewing of stones." And God pardoned her and said: "Don't live like that anymore in the future."

With that, the story is at the end. (Typical Finish ending of Fairy Tales—like "The End" after movies.)

What could one learn first in The Certificate:
That both parents of the hero are blind (lack of consciousness), cannot cook (are not autonomous to provide for their basic, instinctive needs), and the hero nourishes them (like he is the parent of small children; the roles are inverted, and the hero appears to justify himself for not growing into maturity because of that task he has embraced.) Until he "felt tired" and thought it would be better to have a wife to cook him soup (desiring to meet a woman to nourish him—which his mother and father had not done—physically and emotionally). At this point, the hero is certainly not developed enough.

Then, he meets the old man (a prefiguration of the numinous, of God himself) who gives him a stick (a phallic symbol announcing his development into puberty, and in another way, a wooden symbol of the feminine). He did not think about that stick until he got hungry. He saw the stick as he had seen the feminine—a worthless object.

Now, feeling a new type of hunger, the hero starts looking at the new phase of his life and then, the stick "becomes the feminine presence." A girl stood at the roadside: the journey will start. But that wife given by God is not in a hurry "to go to marriage." She says that he must first bring her to his parents. It looks like she desires to meet his previous generation, to know him better, to see where his psyche comes from. But more importantly: she needs the time to be considered more than a maker of soup.

Then, they went to mother and father, stayed together, and got "a farm with servants and all necessary things"—which appears to be an additional gift from the numinous, with which the girl is associated, receiving spiritual power from it. She also represents Mother Earth in its generosity. In fact, the woman was beautiful and gave all beggars help—like a benevolent presence.

We see that what was seriously missing at the beginning—the feminine presence (warmth, beauty, sensibility, generosity) not obtained from the hero's blind mother, is now active. As a matter of fact, in the beginning, both emperor and the hero want to have a wife—but only the hero gets a wife from God. The emperor is envious and will try to obtain that feminine presence he misses inside his own life and self by force. But the anima, who is also numinous, cannot be acquired by force.

One could see the contrast in the next paragraph: The man and his wife welcome the emperor politely, give him food, drinks and gifts—they nourish the hungry emperor—and he threatens the husband, giving him the apparently impossible task of getting the certificate from God, in hopes to obtain his wife. He is a trickster and a robber himself—and possibly represents the current stage of the surrounding culture, which treats women as objects.

The Certificate is also an initiation tale. The hero, showing how human he is, enters a big distress (the shadow). His wife, though, showing how—as a positive aAnima—she belongs more to the numinosity of God than to the emperor's grandiosity, says words we hear at the closing of Christian religious services: "Don't fear anything! Go. I send you." So, *she sends him*, like Jesus sent his Apostles into the world. What a difference between her generous gesture and the one from a negative mother who would try to prevent her son from leaving her to be autonomous in the world. To encourage him, she gives him a sensate function gift of warmth and beauty: her silky scarf, a feminine object. There is a feeling function active here as well, in the gifts they give to the emperor. The wife encourages the hero and demonstrates another function in this fairy tale: her intuition. "Cross yourself on the road," she says, "then the way you have to go opens up." She announces an opening—in a way, her spiritual intuition allows the hero to accomplish his task. With all her beauty and grace, she could remind the reader of a type of Persephone during that dark underworld distress and the numinous power that can be accessed by persecuted people who accept the dark face of God when it shows up (Gandhi could be an example.)

When the hero crosses himself on the road, it reminds us of a ritual in the Christian religion, but this is also a symbol of the union of opposites. As a mature man, he can see both sides of everything now. This could remind one of the myth of Adam and Eve, who wanted to see everything completely, as god does. It can also be reminiscent of Parsifal's vision of the whole, as represented by the Holy Grail, and the myth of humans acquiring fire from the Gods, or the divine vision of the whole. As a Prometheus figure, our hero brings back the certificate, which represents the warmth and light of God (in contrast to "the terrible coldness" God will talk about regarding punishments.) As we go through this tale, one could also be reminded of Odysseus's journey because both narratives represent coming back where one has started and show the hero in his development, confronting the unconscious as his ego searches for the inner source.

People Met by the Hero

Speaking of punishments, one could notice that this tale is also about retribution—a type of initiation to an honest way to live, for the reader and those who hear the story. As we accompany the hero on his journey, we learn about punishments received by the people in which dwellings he spends his evenings. We are encouraged to use our intellectual and logical function, not to act as they did.

The story of the two men who cannot warm their place, of the two women who scoop water out of a ditch, and the old woman who must chew stones day and night is an evident consequence of the everyday human blindness announced by the appearance of the hero's blind parents at the beginning of the tale. The emperor also, as punishment for his actions against the hero, gets blind when the man returns home with his Certificate from God.

One could also learn—because the hero asks God—how the individuals the hero met on his journey can be free from their punishments and obtain wisdom. The hero now acts as an intercessor for these unconscious humans before the divinity, as one of many intercessors we can be reminded of. In the Jewish book of Genesis, for example, Abraham asks God to pardon Sodom and Gomorra, which were about to be destroyed with all its inhabitants. The way Abraham accomplishes his intercessory task is by counting down from fifty people to a single one, Lot, who was considered just—he tried to convince God to pardon the entire city and the region. In fact, in several other ancient spiritual traditions, like Buddhism, forgiveness is believed to be the most important step out of the karmic law.

Symbols and Numbers

The two men (masculine presence) who cannot warm their place: the number two is necessary for a relationship to be possible. In contrast to them, who feel cold, the hero thought their house was too warm. It seems that the problem with these men was that they had a cold heart: "They didn't help any beggar not even in the biggest coldness," God explained. The two women (feminine presence) who endlessly scoop water out of a ditch: again, the number two is necessary for a relationship to be possible. In contrast to them, who complained that they had to scoop water from the ditch for six years, the hero when he drank from the water, found that it was milk. Milk, of course, is connected to what was missing at the beginning of the tale—the female contribution to feed the next generation, in humans and animals. The problem with these women was that "they poured water into the milk they sold" God said. In other words: greed.

The old woman who had chewed stones day and night for twelve years got double the time of the punishment incurred by the two women. One could conclude that the old woman's guilt is heavier. She is alone, and one could interpret that she is a narcissist. The problem with the old woman, God explained to the man, was that "she must chew stones because of her richness with which she did not help anybody who came to ask for it." In other words, her problem was not seeing the other—she would have to chew the rigid stones of her ego, before getting to the presence of God.

In contrast to the old woman, who said she could not give the hero "anything to eat because she had to chew stones day and night," the man gave her his bread, and it became stone in her hands. When she gave him a stone, it became good bread in his hands. Bread has been a staple of nourishment in all cultures since time immemorial. So, here again, the story appears to tell us that what we can have and enjoy depends on the state of our consciousness and the health of our psyche. To try to keep all she had for herself alone (and for a long period; she was old) appears to have brought two times the punishment received by the two women tricksters who poured water into the milk they sold.

One could now consider the way God responded to the man's questions about how these people would get rid of their punishment. The old woman can be free from the hell God has mentioned he could have sent her to when God "let come a big coldness so that the stars fall from the sky. If she can add the stars and tolerate the cold, she can be free." Stars are mirrors of the sun, which is the symbol of God. Regarding the cold, mentioned so many times, we must remember that this is a typical fairy tale from Finland and other countries like Lithuania, Russia, Ukraine—so the cold weather is a big factor.

On the other hand, one could interpret that, perhaps, the translation is not a good one. The old woman needs to "count the stars," instead of "adding" them. In other words: a difficult task. The two women who robbed their clients by pouring water (the unconscious) into the milk they sold will be free "if they count the hairs of their cows in the big coldness" God will send. Another difficult task, which will bring them back to contact with their instinct, and again to the warmth of the female presence missing in the beginning. The two men who complained they could not warm their house will be free when God "sends a horrible coldness that they can stand and add together the stars in the sky."

CONCLUSION

So, the fairy tale The Certificate appears to bring the hero and the heroine to a successful conjunction and the other humans to unification (after being in conflict, the hero and the emperor are at peace; they call each other cousins, meaning they are members of the same human family). The blindness of the beginning—the blind parents of the hero—are now dead, so consciousness has increased from the Jungian point of view.

Even God sings at the funeral for the blindness! The emperor represents the ego and has shown he can learn and evolve. He is, in a sense, that part of the personality that forces the person to go out and has forced the hero to start the glorious journey, where he finds individuation, maturity, a valuable spiritual relationship with God, and obtains the possibility of a pardon for the other humans represented in the story.

NOTES

1. Kast, Verena, Mario Jacoby, and Ingrid Riedel. *Witches, Ogres, and the Devil's Daughter. Encounters with Evil in Fairy Tales* (Boston: Shambhala, 1992), 42.
2. Ibid.
3. Ibid.
4. Ibid.
5. Frey-Rohn, L. *From Freud to Jung: Comparative Study of the Psychology of the Unconscious* (Boston: Shambhala, 1990).
6. Ibid.
7. Tillich, Paul. *Theology of Culture* (New York: Oxford University Press, 1964).
8. Eliade, Mircea. *Images and Symbols*. Studies in Religious Symbolism (New York: Princeton University Press), 11–14.
9. Jung, C. G. *Collected Works* (Princeton, NJ: Princeton University Press, 1944), 130, 148, 400.
10. Ibid.
11. Edinger, Edward. *Ego and Archetype* (Boston: Shambhala Publications, 1972), 178.
12. Ibid.
13. Jung, C. G. *Collected Works* (Princeton NJ: Princeton University Press, 1944), 130, 148, 400.
14. Ulanov, Ann, and Barry Ulanov. *Cinderella and Her Sisters: The Envied and the Envying* (Philadelphia: Westminster Press, 1983).
15. Ibid.
16. Aarne, Antti, and Stith Thompson. *The Types of the Folktale* (Helsinki: Suomalainen Tiedakademia, 1981).
17. Ibid.
18. Ibid.
19. Ibid.
20. Jung, C. G. *Collected Works* (Princeton, NJ: Princeton University Press, 1944), 130, 148, 400.
21. Kast, Serena, Mario Jacoby, and Ingrid Riedel. *Witches, Ogres, and the Devil's Daughter: Encounters with Evil in Fairy Tales* (Boston: Shambhala, 1992), 42.
22. Ibid.
23. Aarne, Antti, and Stith Thompson. *The Types of the Folktale* (Helsinki: Suomalainen Tiedakademia, 1981).
24. Ibid.

Chapter 7

Groundbreaking Neuroscience

Contemporary Contributions to the Process of Analysis

In this chapter, the author will address the work of some significant neuroscientists who belong to more recent cohorts and have promoted development in the process of analysis. These researchers have specifically studied metaphor and its fundamental function both in clinical practice and in poetry.

Based on modern cognitive neuroscience, sustained by their day-to-day clinical experience and carried by contemporary theories of analytic interpretation, Jeanine M. Vivona, Thomas H. Ogden, Antal F. Borberly, and Mark Winborn—among others—demonstrate the transformational power of the metaphor not only in the area of creating art and being healed by poetry but in the progress of individuation which happens in the analytical setting.

In summarizing the impact of these remarks, the author will refer to several titles that may enrich the reader's acquired information about the matter. The research referred to in this chapter was published recently.

THE TRANSFORMING POTENTIAL OF SPOKEN LANGUAGE

Jeanine Marie Vivona (2003), in particular, in her paper "Embracing Figures of Speech: The Transformative Potential of Spoken Language," points out that "Psychoanalysis mobilizes the potentials of language that we admire in poetry."[1]

She draws on H. Loewald's theory of language and therapeutic action to "elaborate two related senses in which psychoanalytic work requires embracing figures of speech."[2]

The scientist clarifies that: "First, language's inherent but frequently unacknowledged capacity is to embrace different modes of experience, particularly verbal and sensorimotor experience. Second, the figures or participants of the psychoanalytic conversation must and do embrace each other with speech."[3]

From the point of view of poetry, one could say that the sound of the voice of the person who reads the poem—the metaphor contained in it—the facial and body expressions from the one who reads "embraces" the one who "receives" the poem.

Speech bridges separate individuals, thus enabling interpersonal connection. Examining the operation of spoken language in psychoanalytic treatment with case references, the author illustrates the clinical utility of mobilizing the transformative capacities of the spoken word and concludes that these intrapsychic and interpersonal bridging capacities of language cause the therapeutic action of the talking cure.

Loewald conceived the infant's prelinguistic, primary process state as a primary unity in which "word" is embedded in "thing."[4] Words as sound surround the baby, indistinct from other aspects of experience; the infant is immersed, embedded in a flow of speech that is part and parcel of a global experience within the mother-child field.[5] For the young child, "language is action through words."[6] As the child begins to speak, words take on language functions as they are separated from the global experience while remaining linked to the things they signify, enabling a secondary process.

In fact, the relation of words to things develops from the primary process state of undifferentiation toward the secondary process state of dynamic linkages between distinct entities, a new level of psychic structure. Loewald remarked that this process of separating and linking words and things occurs in childhood within an interpersonal relationship, a vital part of the learning process. The emotional relation to the person from whom the word is learned plays a crucial part in how alive the link between thing and word turns out to be. In development, as in therapy, a lively relationship breathes vitality into words by providing motivation and purpose for speech.[7]

Vivona points out that throughout life, language maintains vital connections between primary and secondary process realms of experience, "although the latter tends to predominate in mature psychic experience, as abstract thought requires the ability to manipulate symbolic objects without regard for the personal sensations and memories with which they are associated."[8] Nevertheless, the sensorimotor state, which Loewald conceived as primary rather than primitive, is not supplanted but remains accessible through words and imbues language with its power, "that original power of words to conjure up things, which is intimately related to physical, sensory-motor events or acts."[9]

Language Is a Hallmark of the Secondary Process and a Bridge to the Primary Process

Regarding psychopathology, Loewald locates its operation and amelioration in language. He affirms that repression ruptures the connection of word and thing such that words take on a life of their own, less likely to evoke the actions, feelings, and somatic states they signify. Conversely, regression reverses the developmental attainment of the separation of word and thing, effectively submerging words into things so that expression occurs primarily in sensorimotor states and actions, including verbal actions, and only secondarily through the semantic content words. The therapist's verbal interpretation, words created within the emotionally alive therapeutic relationship, aims to restore the simultaneous connection and distinctiveness of word and thing. This integration requires that both psychoanalytic participants remain open to experiencing powerful sensorimotor states that can be linked to growth-enhancing words.

In the word, therapist and patient are reconciled. In fact, as Loewald states, "Language is not merely a means of reporting action, it is itself action; the narrative has a dramatic potential of its own."[10]

As the author said earlier, this affirmation could bring to mind Janus, the Greeks' two-faced god, for it becomes necessary to look backward to resolve aspects of experience interfering with individuation and look forward, discerning the direction of psychological progression or movement. That shift can be detected as we recall Merwin's poem *For the Anniversary of My Death*, where the poet says:

> I will no longer
> Find myself in life as in a strange garment.[11]

In the course of his paper, Ogden continues,

> I will look at the ways in which a poem grapples (often with great success) with the challenges of getting into the language the full richness, complexity, and movement of living human experience. In what follows, I will not be offering an analytic interpretation of a poem, nor will I attempt to provide a piece of criticism that treats the analytic session as a literary "text." To do so would sap the vitality of both the poem and the experience in analysis. Instead, I will address the experience of the Frost poem and the analytic experience, each in its own terms.[12]

On the other hand, Ogden urges the reader to read Frost's poem aloud several times before proceeding to his discussion. He explains that Frost'sbest poems come to life through the play of the sounds and meanings of the words in our mouths as we "say the lines." His remarks, of course, are applicable to every significant poem.

In another paper, "Some Thoughts on the Use of Language in Psychoanalysis" published in *Psychoanalytic Dialogues* (1997)—*and under the subtitle "The Ear Does It," Thomas Ogden discusses the function of metaphor. He suggests that "the analytic discourse requires of the analytic pair the development of metaphorical language adequate to the creation of sound and meanings that reflect what it feels like* to think, feel and physically experience (in short, to be alive as a human being to the extent that one is capable) at a given moment. Such use of language is not an inborn capacity—he says—it requires "ear training," which the analyst provides from the first meeting.[13] Ogden observes that the analyst, while avoiding didacticism, is, in a meaningful way, very much like an English teacher in his effort "to enhance the patient's capacity for attunement to the subtlety of language as well as his capacity to use language in a way that more fully captures/creates his thoughts, feelings, perceptions, and so on in the analytic discourse." He says that he is interested in the way people think about and speak about encounters with other people's symbolic expression/creations of the experience of being human. And this, Ogden concludes, directs us to metaphor. "What is it *like* to read this poem?"[14]

Vivona adds: "By linking the transference action, experienced interpersonally, with the conscious, verbally symbolized realm, interpretation potentiates transformation."[15]

The Language Action of Metaphor: Connecting and Differentiating

In that same paper (2003), under the subtitle "The Language Action of Metaphor: Connecting and Differentiating," Vivona remarks that "the sine qua non of psychoanalytic treatment is putting things, especially inner things, into words, especially words spoken to another person."[16]

From Wright (1991), Vivona quotes, "When we come to the expression of inner things and feelings, things that cannot be seen, metaphor is the only linguistic way of giving them form."[17] Children use metaphors liberally and creatively to express thoughts that transcend vocabulary. Necessarily, metaphoric speech contributes actively to the psychoanalytic dialog, as metaphors create a language for unnamed experiences."[18]

One could note that this is exactly what happens in a poem.

In another paper, "Psychoanalysis as Poetry" (2013), Vivona starts her writing by saying:

> Like psychoanalysis, poetry is possible because of the nature of verbal language, particularly its potential to evoke the sensations of lived experience. These potentials are vestiges of the personal, relational context in which language is learned, without which there would be no poetry and no psychoanalysis." In one sense, the work of the analyst is to create language that mobilizes the experiential, memorial, and relational potentials of words, and, in so doing to make a poet out of the patient and out of the analyst so that the two of them can create such language.[19]

In the same paper, Vivona goes on to affirm:

> To my mind, some of the richest discussions of language in psychoanalysis today are those in which we allow poetry to reveal the action of the verbal therapeutic process. Poetry is nothing but words. Yet the undeniable power of poetry to evoke feelings and alter understandings invites comparison with the action of psychoanalysis. For instance, Ogden (1999) and Parsons (2007) identify a source of therapeutic action in the analyst's ability to listen to the patient's speech as to a poem, remaining open to its multisensorial reverberations as sources of meaning.[20]

The multisensorial conversation.

The author would like to bring to this discussion the contributions of psychoanalysis to embodied language research. One could turn to the mirror neuron system and therapeutic process for that. Whether embodiment is located in language or thought or occurs before or after language comprehension, all embodied models propose that the sensorimotor qualities associated with language derive from personal memories.

The mirror neuron system is frequently cited as a plausible neurobiological mechanism for embodiment in the literature on embodied cognition and language. Mirror neuron studies of language have received little attention in the psychoanalytic literature, and some authors have doubted their relevance to psychoanalysis. By contrast, mirror neuron studies of action observation have catalyzed internal intentions and experiences.

Gallese's embodied simulation model has channeled a psychoanalytic understanding of the mirror neuron system. According to Gallese, as one person observes another, the observer's mirror neuron system matches the sensorimotor activations of the other's brain, enabling the observer to share in the internal experience of the other. Embodied simulation provides "an automatic, unconscious, and no inferential understanding of another's actions, intentions, emotions, sensations, and perhaps linguistic expressions. One could hypothesize that such body-related experiential knowledge enables a direct grasping of the sense of the action performed by others and the emotions and sensations they experience."[21] The embodied simulation model proposes that the other's internal experiences can be understood directly and in their own experiential modes, rather than only indirectly through cognitive processes such as inference, which yields cognitive rather than experiential knowledge of another's internal experience.

Applied to the psychoanalytic situation, the embodied simulation model proposes that the analyst's countertransference contains a replica of the patient's internal experience due to the operation of the mirror neuron system. Embodied simulation is thought to enable the analyst to resonate accurately with the patient's experience, to know that experience directly via the somatic resonance of embodied simulation, and to influence that experience through the modulating effects of his or her brain. Prominent theorists, including Olds (2006), Ster (2004), and Siegel (2006)—says Vivona—have invoked the embodied simulation model to suggest the relevance of the mirror neuron system to psychoanalysis.[22]

Although both are theorized to involve the mirror neuron system, the models' embodied simulation and embodied language emphasize distinct mechanisms for understanding the internal experience of another. The embodied simulation model explicitly separates verbal and cognitive understanding from sensorimotor experiencing, whereas the embodied language model explicitly integrates them; the embodied simulation mechanism foregrounds sensorimotor experience without thought and language, whereas embodied language foregrounds sensorimotor experience in language. Moreover, embodied simulation proposes an automatic simulation of the other's sensorimotor activity, whereas embodied language proposes the activation of one's own sensorimotor experiences. The models are not mutually exclusive. However, it is possible that the mirror neuron system subserves both mechanisms and that both operate during psychoanalytic treatment.

If pushed to its theoretical limits, the embodied simulation model proposes a clinical process with problematic implications. It envisions the possibility of a direct experiential connection to the other that is free of thought and language. Indeed, this direct path might suggest a new royal road to the mind of the other. But unlike its predecessors (e.g., the dream, the transference, the countertransference), this royal road does not require verbalization to realize its therapeutic utility and offers only limited opportunities for the analyst's psychology and subjectivity to enter. More than an interpersonal process, embodied simulation is an inter-biological process, not a meeting of minds but a meeting of brains.

In terms of technique, the embodied simulation model might encourage a laissez-faire attitude, as though the mirror neuron system would be an unerring guide to the patient's inner world if analysts would only refrain from interfering with its automatic operation. This way of thinking might be appealing, as it mitigates the uncomfortable uncertainty of relying on a therapeutic method we have understood to be grounded in ambiguous and fallible subjective experience and its dubious verbal expression. It might bolster an analyst's denial of personal contributions to countertransference experiences by shifting causality to the mirror neuron system. It might move psychoanalysis away from considerations of the inner dynamics of patients and analysts by highlighting automatic processes rather than motivated ones, consequently restricting therapeutic consideration of unconscious conflict and conscious verbal insight.

Quinodoz (2003) agrees with Vivona when he says:

> The speaker is addressing his entire person, so implicitly given rise to a form of listening that mobilizes affects and sensation, and arousing fantasies, including bodily fantasies." He adds: "We can now more readily understand why the analyst needs to prioritize the incarnate aspect of language when addressing patients whose lack of internal cohesion makes them anxious: these patients need, precisely, to be heard by an analyst who can listen to them with the whole of his person—thought, feeling, and body combined in a unity—and who will speak to them in a manner that addresses the totality of their person.[23]

Throughout her work, Vivona shows a consistent interest in supporting her theories through modern neuroscience findings. In her paper "Embodied Language in Neuroscience and Psychoanalysis" (2009), she aims to write a detailed review "of research on embodied language in neuroscience and related disciplines, after which the findings are considered in light of diverse views of language in psychoanalysis," specifically the models of the Boston Change Process Study Group, Wilma Bucci, Fonagy and Target, David Olds, and Hans Loewald.[24]

Vivona concludes that

> The juxtaposition of psychoanalytic models with the findings of research on embodied language shows that scientific studies can focus on the psychoanalytic understanding of verbal processes and that integrations with neuroscience neither inherently threaten the traditional psychoanalytic focus on verbal meanings nor reduce the richness and complexity of psychoanalytic theory.[25]

Another significant contribution comes from Thomas H. Ogden, who, for example, in "The Music of What Happens in Poetry and Psychoanalysis," a paper published in the *International Journal of Psycho-Analysis* (1999), presents to the reader "a close reading of a Frost poem and a detailed discussion of an analytic session.[26] Using specific examples from the poem "Acquainted with the Night" (composed in 1928) and from the analytic session, he then offers some thoughts concerning the relationship between the way he listens to the language of the poem and the way he and his patient speak with and listen to one another.[27]

The author illustrates in this reading of the poem and in the way he speaks that he is not primarily engaged in an effort to unearth what lies "behind" the poem's words and symbols or "beneath" the patient's report of a dream or a life event. Instead (or perhaps more accurately, in addition), he attempts to listen to the sound and feel of what's going on," to the music of "what happens," as he says.[28] This is achieved to a significant degree in the analytic setting by means of the analyst attending to his own reverie experience.

One could consider Ogden's perspective as a welcome movement forging away from the frequent tendency of some ill-informed therapists (and other people, of course) who appear to expect that the poem must tell them a story. A story like some type of "news" they could read in a newspaper. The poem, though, does not intend to do that. In its creation, a good poem is exquisitely vaster, more complex, and enriching in an inordinate number of levels than a mere story could be.

As he starts to play his part in "The Music of What Happens," Ogden informs the reader that:

> In this paper, I will be asking the reader to do a somewhat different sort of work from that which other analytic writers and I usually ask of the reader. In the course of this discussion, I will ask the reader to listen to his listening, that is, to listen to the way he listens and hears me listening to an analytic session. I will try to stay out of the reader's way as he or she does this work, and only at the end of the paper will offer some thoughts about what I currently think listening to and saying a poem has to do with listening to and speaking with a patient in analysis.[29]

Before diving into Frost's poem and the session he will refer to from the twelfth year of a process of analysis, Ogden announces a few introductory comments:

> Over the course of the past fifty years—he says—there have been a number of important shifts in the theory and practice of psychoanalysis. Among them is an increasing awareness that the most interesting and productive avenues of analytic inquiry seem no longer to be adequately addressed by the question, "What does that mean?"—that symptom, that set of dream images, that acting out, that rageful response to the sound of the analyst's coughing, and so on.[30]

Similarly, in the case of interpreting poetry, "an inquiry into personal meanings has become inseparable from an understanding of the unconscious intersubjective context in which those meanings are generated. Consequently, the question 'What does that mean?' has gradually expanded in such a way as to increase emphasis on such questions as: 'What's going on here?" 'What's happening between us consciously and unconsciously, and how does that relate to other aspects of the patient's (and the analyst's) past and present experience, both real and imagined?'"[31]

Another vital consequence of that shift in the theory and practice of our work as psychoanalysts is that, more than ever, each therapist and client pair stands as a unique experience, and that specificity ("what's happening between us consciously and unconsciously, and how does that relate to other aspects of the patient's (and the analyst's) past and present experience, both real and imagined?") brings each therapy session to a crucial newness.

Indeed, Ogden continues: "With this shift in our conception of the analytic process comes the need for a commensurate change in how we use language to speak to ourselves and our patients. It seems to me important that we develop a capacity to use language that does justice not only to the task of understanding and interpreting the conscious and unconscious meaning of our patient's experience; in addition, our use of language must be equal to the task of capturing and conveying in words a sense of what it is 'that's going on here' in the intrapsychic and intersubjective life of the analysis, the 'music of what happens' in the analytic relationship."[32]

Ogden further clarifies: "This paper is offered as a contribution both to the understanding of the shift I have mentioned in our understanding of the nature of the analytic process and to the development of our capacity to use language in a way that is adequate to that shift."[33] Ogden continues:

> In the course of this paper I will look at the ways in which a poem grapples (often with great success) with the challenges of getting into the language, the full richness, complexity, and movement of living human experience. In what follows, I will not be offering an analytic interpretation of a poem, nor will I attempt to provide a piece of criticism that treats the analytic session as a literary 'text.' To do so would sap the vitality of both the poem and the experience in analysis. Instead, I will address the experience of the Frost poem and the analytic experience, each in its own terms.[34]

On the other hand, Ogden urges the reader *to read Frost's poem aloud several times* before proceeding to his discussion. He explains that Frost's best poems come to life through the play of the sounds and meanings of the words and the feel of the words in our mouths as we "say the lines." His remarks, of course, are applicable to every significant poem.

In another paper, "Some Thoughts on the Use of Language in Psychoanalysis"—published in *Psychoanalytic Dialogues* (1997)*—and under the subtitle "The Ear Does It," Thomas Ogden discusses the function of metaphor. He suggests that "the analytic discourse requires of the analytic* *pair the development of metaphorical language adequate to the creation of sounds and meanings that reflect what it feels like* to think, feel and physically experience (in short, to be alive as a human being to the extent that one is capable) at a given moment. Such use of language is not an inborn capacity—he says—it requires "ear training" (Pritchard, 1994), which the analyst provides from the first meeting.[35]

Ogden observes that the analyst, while attempting to avoid heavy-handed didacticism, is, in meaningful ways, very much like an English teacher in his efforts "to enhance the patient's capacity for attunement to the subtlety of language as well as his capacity to use language in a way that more fully captures/creates his thoughts, feelings, perceptions, and so on in the analytic discourse."[36] He says that "he is interested in the way people think about and speak about encounters with other people's symbolic expressions/creations of the experience of being human."[37] And this, he concludes, directs us to metaphor. "What is it *like* to read this poem?."[38] Posing this question, says Ogden, "asks us to bring to bear on the poem something new, something not already in the poem, but perhaps suggested by the poem's effect on us. In this way, the poem is actively engaged; we do something with it as opposed to understanding it."[39]

"The question 'What is it like to read this poem?' focuses on *the experience of reading*, the experience of what it feels like to read, to listen to, to be spoken to (or written to) by the speaker/writer." Ogden says that he believes "that there is an important and interesting overlap between the question "What is it like to read this poem?" and the question "What is it like to be with this patient?"[40]

For Brower (1951, 1968), the experience of reading is not most fundamentally a matter of uncovering "coherent patterns" of meaning hidden in the text which must be deciphered, decoded, or explicated; rather, the emphasis is on creating one's own words and sentences with which to describe the present moment created by the collision of author and reader. As important as the process of understanding (in both the psychoanalytic experience and the experience of reading), the process of not "know[ing] too much" is at least as important. "Much better to practice the art of *not* arriving [at precise meaning]."[41]

Antal F. Borbely, in "A Psychoanalytic Concept of Metaphor"—published in the *International Journal of Psycho-Analysis* (1998)—claims that the main aim of his paper is "to suggest that the concept of metaphor belongs neither exclusively to the linguists, nor the philosophers, but ultimately can best be explored by psychoanalysts."[42] In a somewhat different perspective from the papers, we have reviewed so far, Borbely affirms that this is because psychoanalysts "try, as participants observers, to restore lost metaphoricity as a precondition to regaining creativity (responsiveness) previously constrained by neurotic dynamics."[43]

In that preferentially clinical view, Borbely defends his position by quoting Ricoeur (1991), who says: "Metaphor is defined as seeing something in terms of something else."[44] Borbely, then, connects that assertion with psychoanalysis in the following way:

> Psychoanalysis examines the present in terms of the past and the past in terms of the present. It, therefore, relates past and present metaphorically to each other, implying that both metaphor parts change. This view entails broadening the linguistic metaphor concept towards a supralinguistic, here psychoanalytic, one: metaphor is not only a phenomenon of language—its units are not only words but psychodynamics.[45]

With that remark, Borberly means that the units of a metaphor comprise not only the thinking in which it is expressed but also provide insight into how the person who used it experiences relationships and the world.

Indeed, according to Borberly,

> Familiar concepts of psychoanalytic theory are reformulated in the light of this psychoanalytic concept of metaphor. Symptoms are seen as the analysand's damaged ability to metaphorize past and present. Using interpretation, the analyst helps the analysand to restore metaphorical processes that have been interrupted in their flow from the past to the present and from the present to the past.[46]

In chapter 8, "Breaking the Silence,"the author will present the case of a client in her practice who—due to repeated trauma—came to be an example of that work where the analyst helps the analysand progress in a healthy flow from past to present and from present to past.

Truly,

> metaphor restores the polysemy that is lost in neurotic suffering. The metaphorical processes within psychoanalysis are common to all psychoanalytic schools that focus on the analysis of transference. The increasing attention the concept of metaphor is receiving within psychoanalysis is seen as related to a trend in today's science to move from objective categories to experiential ones.[47]

Borberly affirms that "metaphor has been important to poets and philosophers since the time of Aristotle."[48] He clarifies that "Metaphors allow us to conceptualize familiar things in unfamiliar ways and unfamiliar things in familiar ways."[49] He goes on to say:

> Therefore they are intimately connected with all forms of learning and creativity in the arts, the exact sciences, and the human sciences, especially in personality development. While in the linguistic and philosophical literature, there is no full agreement as to what constitutes a metaphor, and while there is much puzzlement about the precise functions of metaphors, an ever-larger volume of publications on these questions attests to the increasing fascination the issue of metaphor elicits today.[50]

Borberly points out that

> building on Rosch's work (1978), Lakoff (1987) considers that in the cognitive sciences, we are witnessing a transition from an objectivist view (categories are objectively given) to experiential realism (the experiencing human being forms categories). In it, thought is seen as embodied and imaginative as opposed to only abstract and aimed at objective truth. Metaphorical thought as imaginative rationality is central to this new scientific outlook.[51]

In his contribution to his psychoanalytic approach to metaphor, Borbely explains

> (1) that the mind functions metaphorically when faced with challenges requiring creativity, (2) that trauma leads to a degradation of metaphorical processes to mere anagogic ones (the 'repetition compulsion'), and (3) that interpretation uses the metaphorical process in the analysand as well as in the analyst in order to restore the diminished metaphor capacity. Further, (4) (the author) highlights a specifically psychoanalytic concept of the *metaphorical process* (situated between the primary and secondary process). Finally, he suggests that (5) the commonality underlying the divergent theories of psychoanalytic schools lies in re-establishing metaphorical connections between developmental events and transference events. Each school uses its own paradigmatic metaphors around which it builds a developmental and transferential theory and a corresponding technique.[52]

Trends in Post-Jungian Perspectives on the Interpretation

Focused on the specificities of clinical interpretation and under the heading "Trends in Post-Jungian Perspectives on Interpretation," Mark Winborn (2019) writes that, with Michael Fordham's (1958) introduction of a new model of individuation—which proposes that individuation begins in utero and continues throughout life—the reductive-synthetic dichotomy in interpretation began to be reevaluated. As the concept of individuation was expanded into a lifelong developmental model, the analyst must cultivate both "backward-" and "forward-looking" perspectives. Fordham (1978) argues that there are few occasions when a sharp contrast between reductive and synthetic approaches can be maintained.[53]

Winborn uses a metaphor to clarify: Like Janus, the Greeks' two-faced god, it became necessary to look backward to resolve aspects of experience interfering with individuation and look forward, discerning the direction of psychological progression or movement.[54]

> Based upon new understandings of synchronicity, infant development, and lifespan development, a contemporary Jungian position has emerged—affirms Winborn—arguing that the maintenance of a reductive-synthetic dichotomy is no longer viable in the analytic setting (e.g., Siegelman, 1994; Jacobi, 1996; Connolly, 2015). This shift has also been accompanied by ideas emerging in the psychoanalytic world that have greater compatibility with Jungian concepts. As Jacobi (1996) frames the issue: "As far as the question of reductive analysis is concerned, I find it less and less meaningful to set 'reductive' against 'symbolic,' 'clinical,' against 'archetypal,' etc." (pg. 396). Similarly, Siegelman (1994, pg. 494) advocates for the adoption of the term "developmental analysis" to take into account the retrospective, contemporaneous, and prospective lenses which are inextricably interwoven throughout any analysis.[55]

Winborn adds, "a position has also emerged that argues against the bifurcation of experience into the personal and archetypal (i.e., collective) domains as Jung advocated in his work."[56]

As an example of Jung's (1953a) position, he quotes: "When the collective psyche is conceived as a personal appendage of the individual, the result is a distortion of the personality, which is almost impossible to deal with. That is why one is strongly recommended to establish a clear distinction between the personal and collective psyche (para 462)."[57]

For Williams (1963), Zinkin (1969, 1979), and Whitmont (1987), the distinction between experiences of the personal unconscious and elements of the collective unconscious has significance and utility on a theoretical level. Still, in practice, they argue that these experiences are indivisible. As Williams (1963) points out, one of the potential dangers of this dichotomization is the reinforcement of splitting tendencies of the psyche: "In Jungian psychology, the conceptual split, though necessary for purposes of exposition, is considered to be undesirable in practice, since it may add to the splitting tendencies already operative in the psyche."[58]

Daniel Stern's *The Interpersonal World of the Infant* (1985) revolutionized psychoanalytic thinking about infant development and therapeutic work with adults. An enduring legacy of Stern's work is the belief that language plays a minor role in infant development. He considers the possibility that the nonverbal realm is organized preverbally—so that meanings may be known and not spoken or spoken and not known.[59] By contrast, recent research demonstrates that infants use others' spoken words to communicate. Vivona (2006), for example, in her paper "From Developmental Metaphor to Development Model: The Shrinking Role of Language in the Talking Cure" contradicts Stern's position as an exaggeration of the abstract disembodied qualities of language.[60] She contends, "Language can and does evoke and even create a mutative affective and interpersonal experience; that is, the clinical data suggest that the verbal and the nonverbal realms of experience are not inherently disconnected."[61]

EMBODIED LANGUAGE IN NEUROSCIENCE AND PSYCHOANALYSIS

From a recent paper by Jeanine Vivona (2009), one could conclude that many recent studies, particularly in neuroscience, have investigated motoric components to comprehension of language describing bodily action.[62] These studies address the theory that the meaning of action words is represented, in part, in the cortical network involved in the execution of the action, particularly the motor and premotor cortexes; thus, neural processing of language comprehension involves both traditional language regions and modal regions. Studies of the mirror neuron system are an important source of evidence for embodied models, as they suggest a neural mechanism for the motor resonance theorized to underlie action language.[63]

Mirror neurons were discovered in the premotor cortex of the macaque monkey in the early 1990s.[64] The premotor cortex is involved in planning and coordinating motor behaviors, whereas the primary motor cortex is involved in motor performance. Mirror neurons are a unique type of motor neuron, which discharge when a monkey engages in an object-oriented action, such as grasping a banana, and when the monkey observes another individual engaged in a similar action.[65] Although mirror neurons have not been discovered in the human brain, brain imaging studies support the theory that the human brain has a mirror neuron system similar to the operation of actual mirror neurons in the macaque. There is evidence, for instance, that observation of another's object-directed actions stimulates associated regions of the premotor cortex of the human brain.[66] Compared with the activation of mirror neurons in monkeys, the human mirror neuron system appears to be activated by a broader range of stimuli, including language.

Neuroscientists are documenting that the mirror neuron system responds to verbally described actions as it does to observed actions. Using fMRI, researchers have demonstrated that the premotor cortex is activated when participants listen to sentences describing object-directed actions of others (e.g., He is sweeping with a broom) and self (e.g., I grasp a knife).[67] Consistent with the researchers' hypotheses, mirror neuron system activations are similar to those obtained during action observation and greater than those stimulated by listening to sentences with abstract content (e.g., I appreciate sincerity).[68] Similar results have been obtained from studies of silent reading. Aziz-Zadeh et al. (2006) reported that reading phrases describing object-directed actions with mouth, foot, or hand (e.g., grasping the pen) activated the same region of the left premotor cortex as viewing videos of those actions. Similarly, Hauk, Johnsrude, and Pulvermüller (2004) found that reading verbs for hand, foot, and mouth actions (e.g., pick, kick, lick, respectively) differentially stimulated regions of the primary motor cortex and the premotor cortex that closely correspond to regions both stimulated by observation of another's hand, foot, or mouth action and involved in execution of such actions; however, in some studies (e.g., Tettamanti et al. 2005) the primary motor cortex was not activated by linguistically described action. Using PET, Vigliocco et al. (2006) found that nouns and verbs indicating motion events (e.g., *the twirl, it gallops*) and sensory events (e.g., *the darkness, it shines*) differentially activated both modality-specific brain regions, with motion words specifically activating the motor cortex but not the premotor cortex, and brain regions known to be involved in semantic processing (e.g., the left inferior frontal gyrus).[69]

Researchers interpret their findings as consistent with the view that sensorimotor activation is an important component of language comprehension. Tettamanti and colleagues (2005) conclude that their findings support embodied rather than modal theories of action-related language: "In this domain, language does not appear to be detached from the evolutionary ancient sensorimotor system, but rather strictly linked to it."[70] Aziz-Zadeh and colleagues (2006) also highlight the role of the mirror neuron system in sensorimotor reenactments associated with this type of language: "Congruence between the cortical sectors activated by observing actions and re-enactment of sensory-motor representations during conceptual processing of linguistic phrases describing actions."[71]

NOTES

1. Vivona, J. M. "Embracing Figures of Speech: The Transformative Potential of Spoken Language" (*Psychoanalytic Psychology* 20, no. 1, 2003).
2. Ibid.
3. Ibid.
4. Ibid.
5. Ibid.
6. Ibid.

7. Ibid.
8. Ibid.
9. Ibid.
10. Ibid.
11. Merwin, W. S. "For the Anniversary of my Death." *The Second Four Books of Poems* (Port Townsend, WA: Copper Canyon Press, 1992).
12. Ogden, T. H. "Some Thoughts on the Use of Language in Psychoanalysis" (*Psychoanalytic Dialogues* 7, 1997): 1–21.
13. Ogden, T. H. "The Music of What Happens in Poetry and Psychoanalysis" (*International Journal of Psychoanalysis* 80, 1999): 979–94.
14. Ibid.
15. Vivona, J. M. "Embracing Figures of Speech: The Transformative Potential of Spoken Language" (*Psychoanalytic Psychology* 20, no. 1, 2003).
16. Ibid.
17. Ibid.
18. Ibid.
19. Vivona, J. M. "Psychoanalysis as Poetry" (*Journal of the American Psychoanalytic Association,* 2013): 1109–37.
20. Ibid.
21. Ibid.
22. Ibid.
23. Ibid.
24. Ibid.
25. Ibid.
26. Ogden, T. H. "The Music of What Happens in Poetry and Psychoanalysis" (*International Journal of Psychoanalysis* 80, 1999): 979–94.
27. Ibid.
28. Ibid.
29. Ibid.
30. Ibid.
31. Ibid.
32. Ibid.
33. Ibid.
34. Ibid.
35. Ogden, T. H. "Some Thoughts on the Use of Language in Psychoanalysis" (*Psychoanalytic Dialogues* 7, 1997): 1–21.
36. Ibid.
37. Ibid.
38. Ibid.
39. Ibid.
40. Ibid.
41. Ibid.
42. Borbely, A. "A Psychoanalytic Concept of Metaphor" (*International Journal of Psychoanalysis* 79, 1998): 923–36.
43. Ibid.

44. Ibid.
45. Ibid.
46. Ibid.
47. Ibid.
48. Ibid.
49. Ibid.
50. Ibid.
51. Ibid.
52. Ibid.
53. Winborn, M. "Interpretation in Jungian Analysis." (New York: *Art and Technique,* 2019), 21.
54. Ibid.
55. Ibid.
56. Ibid.
57. Ibid.
58. Ibid.
59. Ibid.
60. Vivona, J. M. "From Developmental Metaphor to Development Model: The Shrinking Role of Language in the Talking Cure" (*Journal of the American Psychoanalytic Association* 54, 2006): 894.
61. Ibid.
62. Ibid.
63. Ibid.
64. Ibid.
65. Ibid.
66. Ibid.
67. Ibid.
68. Ibid.
69. Ibid.
70. Ibid.
71. Ibid.

Chapter 8

Breaking the Silence

Metaphor in My Practice

The American poet Adrienne Rich (1929–2012) famously wrote in 1995:

> Every poem breaks a silence that had to be overcome.[1]

Encouraging poets to prevail over silence, Rich says: "What poetry is made of is so old, so familiar, that it's easy to forget that it's not just the words, but polyrhythmic sounds, speech in its first prismatic meanings lit by each other's light, stained by each other's shadows."[2]

In this chapter, giving the reader examples of metaphor in her practice as an analyst, the author will suggest that, in psychoanalytic practice, a deep silence—sometimes coming from previous silenced generations—must be overcome. When it finally finds its voice, that silence, like in writing poems, is frequently expressed in metaphor.

In the unprecedented time of the COVID-19 pandemic, it is remarkable that more and more people found solace in reading and sharing poems. For instance, the Academy of American Poets launched "Shelter in Poems," an initiative that invited poets and poetry lovers to share poems on social media to obtain comfort and courage.

Frequently read at graduations and significant moments of transition, poem "blessing the boats" by the American poet Lucille Clifton (1936–2010), could be shared in an analytical session the same way as Thomas Ogden tells us he shares the poem "Acquainted with the Night," composed by Frost, with his clients.

In this chapter, the author will offer examples of significant metaphors in her practice, which opened new dimensions to therapeutic work progress with clients. Although evidently numerous important images surface in each case, she will offer examples of significant metaphors in her practice, which opened new dimensions to therapeutic cases, one could refer to only a few of them. More importantly, the author will try to share them from a point of view analogous to Thomas Ogden's, when he talks about the relationship between the way he listens to the language of a poem and how he and his patient speak with and listen to one another. Meaning that the analyst is not primarily engaged in an effort to unearth what lies "behind" or "beneath" the patient's report of a dream or a life event.

Instead—as mentioned in chapter 7—Ogden attempts to listen to the sound and feel of what is going on, to the music of what happens. This is achieved to a significant degree in the analytic process by the analyst attending to his or her own reverie experience. And one could say—connecting it to Clifton's poem—that "*beyond the face of fear*," analysand and analyst experience sailing "*through this to that*."[3] In his paper, Ogden offers what he thinks listening and saying a poem has to do with listening to and speaking with a patient in analysis.

In fact, the analytical process has shifted in the past fifty years, and the "What does this mean?" question has been expanded to "What's going on here?" Ogden clarifies that question in the following way: "What is happening between us consciously and unconsciously, and how does that relate to other aspects of the patient's (and the analyst's) past and present experience, both real and imagined?"[4] That shift brings us to a necessary change in how we use language to speak to ourselves and to our patients—in an analogous way that we may process a poem, a metaphor.

Ogden proposes that our use of language must convey in words "a sense of what is going on here" in the intrapsychic and intersubjective life of the analysis, what he calls "the music of what happens in the analytic relationship."[5]

In the following paragraphs of this chapter, one will be able to visit some examples of *sailing through this to that* in the analytical process, as the clients and the analyst go through metaphors, rhythms, and embodiment—as we listen to the poem we are composing together. In the same direction as Lucile Clifton proposes "*poetry is a way of living in the world*."[6]

ON THE MUSIC OF METAPHOR—1

We will call her Ulla. She came for analysis as a forty-one-year-old female, married, mother of one daughter, and her main complaint revolved around severe anorexic symptoms and, sometimes, bulimic episodes. For instance, late at night, she would sometimes leave home surreptitiously and go to a nearby gas station's convenience store, where she would eat quantities of cookies and other foods available there. Back at home, ashamed of what she had done, Ulla would jump in one place for hours to lose the additional weight she could have acquired. Even when no bulimic episode occurred, she would spend hours at a gym every day and run to the point of exhaustion around a nearby lake. Like other people afflicted by anorexia, Ulla had a secret diet that she was the only one to prepare, and nobody could see her eating.

The first time the author saw her, the analyst felt deeply moved. Extraordinarily thin, with her dark hair rigidly collected behind her head in a bun, she looked much older than she was. As her fair skin appeared barely visible under an oversized dress that concealed her diminishing proportions, one could be reminded that anorexia is often a life-threatening condition. In more severe cases, it is difficult to disentangle the primary psychiatric symptoms from the secondary effects of induced starvation. The author felt that the analytical process they were embarking on at that moment could be a very difficult one. In fact, Ulla presented additional physical symptoms common to anorexics: she complained of depression, cold intolerance, some form of alopecia, severe cardiovascular problems, and, as a consequence of starvation, her daughter was born a tiny, premature baby. But the more severe issues would surface later.

The Mirror

When she started treatment, Ulla was terrified of *looking at herself in a mirror*. When the analyst and Ulla had a Skype session, for instance, the client needed to put a piece of paper over her picture on the screen—so she would not see herself. At the start of therapy, she complained that she could not comb her hair because she could not muster the courage to look at a mirror. If she were about to enter a room where she sensed there was a mirror, she would refuse to go into that place.

In a type of reverie, as the author listened to that client talk about her enthusiasm toward a Christmas tree in the first session (which reminded the analyst of the image of an evergreen that survives challenging winters), she silently asked herself: What is going on here? One could hypothesize that there was a lot of aggression that Ulla was turning against herself—because of the evident risk she was inflicting on her own life as she refused to eat sufficiently—but what was it like to fear directly looking at herself in a mirror?

At that point, a few lines by the Japanese poet Basho came to the psychoanalyst's mind:

> Which tree does it come from,
> that fragrance.[7]

One could have been reminded of being back in São Paulo, seeking the wonderful fragrance of the guavas in her aunt's backyard—as I described to the reader in the poem included in the preface of this book. To find out what was going on by discerning the guavas' fragrance in the intrapsychic and intersubjective life of the analysis (what Ogden calls the "music of what happens" in the analytic relationship) appeared to be a good enough direction to follow at that point.[8]

Indeed, bit by bit and working together, the client and her analyst started discerning how Ulla's massive panic reaction at the possibility of seeing herself in a mirror represented a metaphor reflecting her situation. A mirror—or even the picture of her face, which could be visible to her on her computer—confronted her with one of her inner images, something she was horrified to look at.

Anorexia, as we know, is very frequently associated with trauma in mother-daughter relationships. In Ulla's case, that situation was blatant. When she was eleven years old, for instance, her mother—who had been a woman admired for her beauty—decided to put Ulla on a diet because "she was too fat." Looking at the pictures the client brought to the session, though, the child did not need a diet at that age. The mother did. That mother who had started competing with her beautiful daughter used to beat her viciously. For instance, if the child called her, she would scream: "If you do not stop calling me immediately, I will get to where you are and snatch away the skin off your face!" Throughout these episodes and many similar others, the preservation of the client's image and identity—as well as her physical body—was in danger.

On the other hand, there was a continuous vacuum regarding a father's presence, as he always supported whatever the mother determined. Indeed, when Ulla was a small child, she would go to bed with a knife "to protect herself, in case a robber would enter the house during the night," the client explained. In our analytical process, we came to understand that gesture metaphorically expressing that Ulla was being robbed of what a child needs and was not receiving.

Little by little, and as a result of our analytical process of "sailing from this to that," we began to discern that what caused the client massive panic, in case she dared look at a mirror, was the image of her inner mother. That accusing, invasive, jealous inner mother felt like a living monster inside Ulla. For that reason, her image in a mirror—which was also Ulla's image—was seen as capable of destroying the daughter. Ulla could not confront her.

That panic was certainly dramatic at the very beginning of their work together. As the sessions continued, though—and she never missed a session, and is always on time—Ulla worked diligently in her inner world, appearing to make progress.

She has been in therapy with the author for over seven years. Currently, she has no problem looking at herself in a mirror. Based on her own discernment, she decided to go to the gym only twice a week. She successfully defended her PhD thesis—a project she could not accomplish before coming to analysis—and is now employed as a university professor. She also teaches courses on Spinoza and other philosophers online. Most of all, the client has improved her sense of inner authority and—despite her still serious defenses—appears to start discovering connection links in her inner world experience.

In concluding the mirror metaphor's observations, one could describe a pivotal moment in this client's case.

When Ulla was very young, she fell in love with her sister's boyfriend at the time, and they had sexual encounters for years—Ulla desired that he would stay with her, but the young man did not agree with that. This continued relationship caused deep trouble in her relationship with her family. Recently, as her husband left home, Ulla tried to rekindle the contact with that person. The man appeared to be ready to go to bed with her, but nothing that would imply stability. She tried to affirm to herself how vital that relationship had been in her life. Then, she wrote a letter to him, revealing how meaningful the relationship had been for her. The man did not answer. She called him and discovered that he was now scared by what she had written to him instead of appreciating her feelings and trust.

Some hours later, walking by herself and entering an elevator that had a big *mirror* inside, Ulla exclaimed, *looking directly into the mirror*: "What a big fantasy! *I am too complex for that person!* He would never be able to understand me, let alone love me. What was I doing, agonizing for him to call me? What do I gain by doing that?!"

This moment was a pivotal one for Ulla: she had discovered her reflective consciousness. This inner move was a promising evolution in the mirror metaphor she had brought with her. She had found her voice—which had been hidden from the jealous wrath of the terrible mother. Ulla had discovered in the mirror the reflection of a stronger, mature woman with the strength to confront the lies of the negative mother archetype.

The Flood

If the reader encountered the metaphor "*The changes came like a tidal wave*" in a poem or heard it as part of a client's dream, one would probably see an image in their mind representing a powerful wave. At the beginning of our work together (for around five months), Ulla used to bring a flood of dreams to the session: sometimes ten or more long dreams, which we would not have time enough to address during the hour. Many of these dreams were about catastrophic flooding.

In a frequent example, the client would describe a tsunami coming into the building where she was and invading the place. Ulla would swim toward the ceiling, getting cornered there by the water, and be scared that she would drown. In a similar dream, the ocean "overflows" and invades a place where a party is in progress. In another example, after being scared of seeing clowns at the Carnival Festival in Rio (she had always been terrified by clowns and their masks), she must walk on foot through a lagoon (near her parents' home) with her father. As they proceed, fishes and eels swim between their legs. The client is terrified by these and thinks, in the dream, that a giant serpent can appear also. In that dream, the father informs her that there is no danger because the snake only attacks at night, and they are walking across the lagoon during the day.

As Lucille Clifton said, "poetry is a way of living in the world," which can be associated to the analyst's reverie in the analytical hour.[9] As the author heard that dream, a possible connection relating the fishes and eels swimming between the father's and daughter's legs—an event that felt very dangerous to the dreamer—appeared to announce a possible constellation of an unresolved Oedipal complex regarding the father and being expressed as a fear of violation. I did not think that Ulla was ready to hear this interpretation yet, though. Later on, when we visit another pivotal metaphor moment in this client's analysis, this hypothesis will be addressed.

As the work evolved, more and more flood nightmares were brought to the session until around eight months later. Then, the author invited Ulla to participate in the Association Experiment (a Jungian practice to bring unconscious elements to consciousness). A dramatic incestuous recurrent event in her family life was then revealed. Indeed, nature is more powerful and much older than human beings. As long as we live, we are surrounded by nature. At the same time, we are part of it." Thus, stories of deluges are found everywhere, like in the cosmic flood described in Genesis 7:11, where "all the fountains of the deep burst forth, and the windows of heaven were opened," but Noah, his family, and animals were saved. Earlier than the Biblical story, there is a Sumerian version of the great deluge, the *Epic of Atrahasis*. In the Babylonian *Epic of Gilgamesh*, the hero rides out a cosmic flood with his family and animals and comes to rest, as Noah does, on a mountaintop. Any heavy rainfall may share some of the deluge's symbolism.

As a metaphor for unconscious energy, the waters' lunar power may announce the end of a cycle and the beginning of a new one. It may cause death but also regeneration. In fact, in *Anatomy of the Psyche*, Edward Edinger suggests that Alchemy intuited in the image of the flood the dissolution of psychic structures that no longer serve the self's integrity.

Edinger says: "The greater *solutio* is an encounter with the Numinosum, which both tests and establishes the ego's relation to the Self. What is worth saving in the ego is saved. What is not worth saving is dissolved and melted down in order to be recast in new life forms."[10]

In Ulla's case, the flood nightmares appeared to be connected to physical and emotional confusion generated by an early incestuous reality in her life. For years, the whole family—both parents, her sister, and herself—were brought to sexually interact, at the same time, in the parents' bed, embracing, caressing, and kissing each other as instructed by the mother, who delighted in instigating the recurrent event. Physical and emotional confusion surrounding the child—as one could come to see in the analytical process—are visible in the metaphor of the floods assailing the dreamer. The tsunami represented the situation where there was no safe ground under the feet amid the churning of the deep waters. Ulla's ego feared being invaded and drowned in catastrophic floods.

On the other hand, one could remember that the young child used to go to bed with a knife "to protect herself, in case a robber would enter the house during the night." Indeed, she *was* being robbed. She was also terrified to see clowns in the streets during Carnival. Clowns can be reminiscent, in their symbolic appearance, of the traditional traumatic image—they are part of the libretto in many operas—concealed underneath their masks. Indeed, a very different reality from the perfect family and perfect parents the client was convinced to believe she was raised by.

Not surprisingly, Ulla was very late to start developing boundaries (an absence of which is also certainly related to her inclination to promiscuity as a young woman) and only recently started to experience her own reflective consciousness.

The Client Kisses Her Father at the Bottom of the Ocean

In a more recent dream, Ulla goes into the ocean with her father. As one might know, the sea is a universal metaphor for the deepest unconscious. Before entering the waters, in the dream, the father complains to her that he cannot see clearly. As they come to the waves and reach the bottom of the ocean, the father looks at her and exclaims: "Now I can see clearly. You are *so pretty*!" And, in the dream, Ulla seductively kisses her father's lips. The reader may hypothesize that the client's psyche can now present to her consciousness one of her secret conflicts, which has harassed her for her entire life: the unresolved Oedipal relationship with her father. Like in the Oedipus myth, Ulla's dream expresses a powerful metaphor surfacing from the process we had been "sailing through." Ulla's father—in her dream, as in real life, as a not good enough father—*cannot see*.

On the other hand, the metaphor in Ulla's dream goes beyond her personal father's complex boundaries. Indeed, that dream happened when the client had repeatedly sent the author, outside of their regular hours, constant long emails asking for advice which she characterized as "your kind assistance," "your valuable opinion," etc. The author thought that her requests should be discussed during their weekly sessions. Because Ulla was navigating a complicated divorce, though and the analyst was aware of the emergency she was going through, she emailed the client back each time. Of course, it took her inordinate time not only to read her long, anxious narratives but mainly to compose a clear, objective response to her dilemmas. The client received these responses, and benefited from them, but never thanked the author for the time and effort to give her extra time for free outside of their contract.

In the metaphor, we are presented in the dream—expressed as a seductive kiss on her father's lips at the bottom of the unconscious—we can also recognize a metaphor in Ulla's behavior toward the analyst. Indeed, the client had been unconsciously trying to obtain free time consultation—outside of their contract—and disguising her request as a quick question about advice and opinion. Here again, we are confronted with the metaphor of the clown's mask she was so afraid of. Interestingly, the client commented that while she was a child, there were panels of masks hanging from several walls in her home. They were her mother's work, who produced them to be sold as artistic decorations.

As she navigated her emotionally alive work process, Ulla's flood nightmares disappeared. Indeed, more recently, Ulla dreamed that she and the analyst were having an analytical session at the beach. She was sitting on the sand, and the author was in the ocean. As she described her dream, she cleverly remarked: I was having a dream inside a dream! She noticed that she was paying attention to the dream she was telling the analyst (in the dream) and then suddenly noticed that the author was drowning. She appeared to be sorry that she did not realize that before—as she was only focused on herself. She then sprinted into the ocean and saved her analyst from the waves. The author understood that now the client was able to save herself from the flood. In the beginning, she had possibly sensed a risk that the intensity of the flood of her unconscious material could drown her analyst. In that recent dream, symbolically, by saving the author from the waves, one could say that Ulla saved herself, her analyst, and her analysis process.

ON THE MUSIC OF METAPHOR—2

The next metaphors come as moments of music and consciousness in the analytical process with another client. One could call him Bruce. A forty-eight-year-old male, married twice, and the father of two adolescents, eighteen and fifteen years old, Bruce, who is currently separated, had both children with his first wife, Sharon, whom he describes as "not a great wife but an excellent mother."

Bruce came to therapy because of his trouble remaining asleep during the night. He would wake, get up, and, unable to get back to sleep, watch television. When his therapy started, the client worked as an Uber driver, so the lack of regular bedtime during the night appeared to be a potential danger to himself and his passengers. He also wanted to discuss his marital relationships and the lack of a more desirable job.

The client was born into a middle-class family. His mother—thirteen years younger than his father—was originally from Athens, Greece, and the father, born in Pittsburgh, was one of ten children of a Syrian family from Damascus. The family belongs to the Orthodox Greek Church, where the father—fifty years old at Bruce's birth—was very active. The client was the younger of four children: three brothers and one sister. In his youth, Bruce had the intention to complete his training as a physician and, with that aim, attended the first years of biology in Pittsburgh. He left his studies to work with his older brothers and father in stock investment. With the 2008 crisis, though, Bruce and his father and brothers suffered devastating financial losses. The client told the author that he had $3 million and lost that sum. On the other hand, the client, who claims he enjoyed exceptional times with his brothers and was very close to them, lost both of them: one to suicide, and the other, in mysterious circumstances that can be seen as an unconscious self-inflicted death as well.

According to Bruce, his brother Michael—one year older than him—lost millions of dollars in stocks, remortgaged his house, borrowed money from the client, and lost all these funds because he reinvested them in shares. He was found dead by his wife, poisoned by his car's fumes, in their home's garage. The brother left behind his wife and two adolescent children. Bruce was called to take care of the situation in the remaining family.

Some years earlier, his other brother, Phillip—five years older than Bruce—was also found dead. He was active, among other activities, in the slot machine business. He performed that work for a type of Mafia organization where the members could only position their devices in the territories assigned to them. Bruce's brother turned a blind eye to that virtual boundary and started placing his machines in places set for others. He was found dead in his mountain cabin—the narrative being that he had killed himself. The problem with that version is that the gun's wound, located on the back of his head, contradicts the feasible way that a person could commit suicide. In his attempt to find out what had happened, Bruce dealt with the police about the case for years. Still, the identity of the perpetrators or the motives for the crime were never clarified.

The client told the author that, since his two brothers' death, his father became depressed and suffered three heart attacks, which made him unable to move, and spent the rest of his life watching TV. At that point, the line from Basho's poem started to blink in the psychoanalyst's mind: "I don't know which tree it comes from, that fragrance."

Then, the client reported the following metaphor: "When my brothers were alive, things were happy, exciting. Then, there is a hole in your heart." His sister, Calliope, fifty-three, who lives in another city, has a close relationship with him. "Cali is warm—he says—we can laugh together about bad times." In another metaphor, he offers: "Her baby grandson, three months old Michael, is a ray of sunshine."

Bruce started his first session in analysis by telling the author that he needed help with not being able to go back to sleep at night, which proved to be a recurrent topic throughout their work. Although the author suggested that scientific research recommends not watching TV close to going to bed because this creates activity in the brain, which makes it difficult to fall asleep, the client kept watching sports clips during the night and never moved the TV from his bedroom. During their work together, as the two of them "sailed from this to that" in composing their analytical poem, the analyst considered constantly his client's lack of willingness to separate from his TV set.

The author also hypothesized that a person with so many painful experiences with death and his specific emotional characteristics (more on this later) would probably equate sleep with losing control and, perhaps, even experiencing nightmares—although Bruce pointed out that he never dreams and does not recall ever having dreamed. On the other hand, because the client, on our first session, associated remaining awake to a recollection of his father ("I watch TV as my father did"), one could connect that to the idea that staying awake during the night and watching TV could be unconsciously felt like being in connection with his father—a metaphor.

Asked about his relationship with Phillip Senior, Bruce was proud to say that his father was a war hero. He received a Purple Heart for having fought in the Boers' Battle in Belgium—one of the most dangerous battles, he explains.

After the end of the war, Bruce continues, his father went to Harvard on the G.I. Bill, and graduated as a history professor. Then, he started his stock business on the side and owned several companies, including shopping centers. Soon, the client's father had forty stockbrokers working for him. Then, when the crisis came, he lost all his business. After he could not walk or move anymore, he watched TV sitting on a chair or in bed because of the stroke. When he would see war films on TV, he would cry, says Bruce, revealing that his father had been awarded many medals. At his funeral, the flag was around his coffin, and he was deeply involved with church and politicians—"very proactive for the underdog," the client clarifies.

Regarding typology, Bruce was extroverted and a sensate type. He coaches his son's baseball team, describes images from his fantasies well—which will be demonstrated later—and is frequently flirtatious. The client appreciates the fantastic imagery displayed in Orthodox churches, although he is not religious. And he does not enjoy being a salesman—a job he obtained after starting therapy—given that he finds the work repetitive.

Regarding his marriages, the client complains that his second wife—who happened to have the same name as the first, and Bruce calls her "S" to differentiate from the first—is not a maternal person. That second wife left him a few months before he started therapy, taking the dog and the cat with her. Bruce observes that animals are innocent and that he misses them much more than the presence of "S." "The dog was Sally, and the cat was Bella," he clarifies.

As they advanced in their analytical process, or the creation of the poem of their relationship, the author noticed that the unconscious content that Bruce brought to their conversation looked very much like the characterization of a type called *puer aeternus,* the eternal male child—a metaphor in itself. The words *puer aeternus* come from Ovid's *Metamorphoses* (another suggestion of the transformative power of poetry) and are applied to a child god in the Eleusinian mysteries.

Ovid speaks of the child-god Iacchus, addressing him as *puer aeternus* and praising him for his role in these mysteries. The title *puer aeternus*, in its translation from Latin, means eternal youth. Still, the expression is also used to indicate a specific type of young man who has an outstanding mother complex and who, accordingly, behaves in specific typical ways. In general, the man identified as *puer aeternus* remains too long in adolescent psychology; that is, all those characteristics distinctive in a youth of seventeen or eighteen are continued into later life, coupled in most cases with significant dependence on the mother. In that case, the mother's image—the portrait of the perfect woman who will give everything to a man and who is without any shortcomings—is sought in every feminine figure. Analysts frequently say that such a man is looking for a mother goddess so that each time he is fascinated by a woman, he later must discover that she is an ordinary human being. Once he has been in an intimate relationship with her, the whole fascination vanishes, and he turns away disappointed, only to project the image anew onto one woman after another.

This situation leads to a form of neurosis, which H. G. Baynes has described as the "provisional life," that is, "the strange attitude and feeling that one is *not yet* in real life. For the time being, one is doing this or that, but whether it is a woman or a job, it is *not yet* what is really wanted, and there is always the fantasy that sometime in the future, the real thing will come about. If this attitude is prolonged, it represents a constant inner refusal to commit oneself to the moment." Indeed, these words illuminate many of Bruce's characteristics. He portrays his mother as *perfect* and shows a preference for women who are maternal figures.

On the other hand, in a similar way as the line in Basho's poem, the author was inclined to admit that we "don't know (yet) which tree it comes from, that fragrance." Meaning the fragrance produced by a few questions connected to the fact that such a *perfect mother* and a respected, *heroic father* have had the misfortune of losing two of their sons to suicide. Are the self-inflicted deaths of the two brothers connected with the "perfect" mother, or is it possible that the tragedy is not primarily rooted in the relationship with the mother but, instead, evokes the father's character?

One could certainly need to know more about the father. That respected, heroic soldier whose voice sounds like "a roaring lion" (as in the metaphor presented by his son) and who, at the end of life, turns into an escape artist (another metaphor; this time, proposed by the author), as he watches TV all day long. Perhaps the father's wound plays an essential role in the many problems and father's complex Bruce has shouldered to analysis. Indeed, as recounted by Bruce, his "father would go to church and invite everybody to go to their home, and then he would go upstairs and watch TV. He never made a meal, did dishes, cleaned the house—old school," the client remarks. "The two roles were evident" for his parents. Based on his description, one could hypothesize that the two brothers' suicides could be more deeply related to the father's overidealized conception of what is real. The mother appeared to have a better connection with reality: people come from church; she serves a meal to all of them and entertains them gladly. In contrast, the father, who invites everybody, goes upstairs and watches TV. With that metaphor, we might be reminded that it is challenging to survive the clash when idealization clashes with reality.

Indeed, considering one of the brothers—the one who was found poisoned by the fumes of his car, in the garage—one could see that he heavily invested funds in the market—funds which were not even his own—and failed to see that the money would not come back. Then, he killed himself. Regarding the brother who was found dead in his cabin in the mountains, one could presume that he judged he was above Mafia law and did not honor reality by choosing to position his coin machines in territories belonging to others.

In his article "Puer Wounds and Ulysses' Scar," published in *Puer Papers,* a book he edited, James Hillman states: "Modern psychology tells us that the parents can be the wounders. Everyone carries a parental wound and has a wounded parent. Today we call these wounds neurosis and work in therapy at healing the parental wounds."[11]

The Extraordinary Wedding Proposals

One could consider two stories that preceded Bruce's two marriages. They will exemplify some of the fantasies Bruce tried to stage in his life, which can be seen as characteristic of a *puer aeternus* personality.

In the first narrative, the client is planning his proposal to his first wife, Sharon. Of course, he loves that girl (or, at least, he thinks he does), and, as a consequence, the whole project must be extraordinary—to be at the same level as his emotion. Having determined his plan, Bruce invites Sharon to go to Paris with him. She accepts. Arrived in Paris, he tells her it will be a great idea to visit the Tour Eiffel. She agrees. And there, on top of the Eiffel Tower, in the heart of Paris, he proposes.

She is surprised, delighted, and they get married, have two kids. It could be a happy, romantic story—and probably, from a certain point of view, it was. But remember the prediction mentioned before: the client appears to be looking for a mother goddess. Even considering the client's peculiarities and being alert to the poetic metaphor in our analytical process, one could witness "something like that" surfacing. When Bruce was fascinated by a woman, he later needs to discover that she is an ordinary human being. Once he had been intimated with her—and, in this case, even dared to commit—the fascination vanished, and he turned away disappointed, only to project the image anew onto one woman after another.

In Bruce's case, it is interesting to notice that he chose a high tower in a city famous for expressing elegance, beauty, and romanticism to lift his proposal. Apparently, his feeling of inferiority needed an established icon of success, a metaphor, up in the air. In fact, during therapy, he proudly said: "Sharon would not find anyone else in the world who would have done this for her!"

The second narrative shows Bruce, already separated from Sharon, waiting for an elevator inside a building. The elevator arrives where the client is standing; the door opens, and, among other people who disembark, there is that girl with a magnificent smile. Bruce looks at her smile, and—ZAZ—he falls in love. (That is precisely the way Bruce told the story to the analyst.)

So, they start a relationship, and Bruce decides he wants to marry her. Again, an excellent opportunity for him to come up with another extraordinary proposal.

By that time, Bruce's two brothers had died. The client had bought the right to have a plaque in one of the benches positioned by the ocean, where he placed a brief eulogy honoring his brother, the one who was closest to him and who, like the other, had committed suicide.

In the second extraordinary proposal, Bruce invites "S" to go with him to the place where that bench was and sit with him to enjoy the view of the ocean. "S" agrees. Inadvertently to her, though, Bruce had arranged that a small plane would fly over the sea, in front of the place they would be sitting, carrying a banner, where it was written: WOULD YOU MARRY ME?

At the stipulated time, Bruce and "S" are sitting on the bench (with the brother's eulogy against their backs), and the small plane flies around with its banner displaying the vital question across the sky. "S" notices the plane, reads the flag, and exclaims: Look, Bruce, how interesting! It is written there: Would you marry me?" Bruce asks: "Would you?!" That's the second extraordinary proposal.

As we already know, the client, nowadays, prefers to have the company of Sally, the dog, and Bella, the cat, instead of the magnificent smile of his second wife, which caused him to fall in love.

What is extremely significant in this tale, though, is (1) that it happens by the ocean—the symbol of the unconscious—(2) that the important message is again "up in the air," like when the client staged his proposal at the top of the Eiffel Tower, and (3) that there is an apparent disconnection here. He is planning to signify a happy, foundational start of a new life together. And at the same time, he stages his proposal in the presence of death via the eulogy honoring his brother, who had committed suicide.

When Bruce—enthusiastically—told the author this story, it sounded like a macabre metaphor to her. But he was unaware of the possible link between the two realities. On the other hand, even if we consider this metaphor chilling—as the analyst felt—the bench with the eulogy engraved on its back has the possibility of unconsciously representing something positive. What is inscribed in it belongs to Bruce's past (on his back), belongs to his reality, and is not forgotten. Observed from that perspective, one could say that, despite the tragedy, the client appears to be able to look forward and start a new relationship, which means to have a future and not to commit suicide.

He could perhaps have developed a more mature personality from his relationship with his mother, whom one could see as more grounded in reality. One could even recall here—in a prose mode—the final lines of "blessing the boats," by Lucille Clifton

Beyond the face of fear, may you kiss the wind then turn from it, certain that it will love your back.

This second interpretation could remind us of what Verena Kast points out in her book *Joy, Inspiration, and Hope:*

> Whereas anxiety drives the individual into isolation—she writes—joy is the foundation of alliance and solidarity. Human beings are both anxious and joyful by nature; we need both solitude and relationships. Individuation requires both parts.[12]

In therapy, the analyst endeavors to strengthen self-esteem. Joy is a strengthening resource that life naturally offers, so it seems meaningful to draw on joy as part of the therapist's efforts at strengthening the ego complex. We need only think of what can happen when we fall in love to imagine the transformative potential of joy.

A Job in a Yacht Going to Exotic Places

One could consider a metaphor in this client's analytical process, which expresses the concept of "provisional life" connected with his *puer aeternus*' personality. It refers to his urge to go away, to not be bound to anything. Indeed, Bruce was brilliant, a superbly gifted type, but he was reduced to menial work because his fantasies did not allow him to be grounded in reality.

Before he came to be the author's client, he had not been stably employed for a long time and drove his car for Uber. One day, one of the passengers he happened to be driving offered him a job on a fantastic yacht that used to cruise to far away, delightful places. Bruce was instantly interested and started asking questions. That person presented himself as the one in charge of the yacht at the dock in South Florida. After inquiring about his driver's academic background, health, family, and disposition, the passenger said he would talk to the owner—a very prosperous man—and recommend Bruce for a job interview.

With that invitation, Bruce's fantasies started flying, and he was making plans. How wonderful that he could go away to these beautiful places for six months or more, earn money, meet interesting people, experience lovely nature, learn new things. And leave behind "S," whose smile had already lost some brilliance at that time.

Bruce and the person in charge of the yacht started talking more frequently. The man wanted Bruce to undergo a medical exam. Bruce agreed and passed the medical exam. Then the man wanted him to buy uniforms for when they would depart on that travel. Bruce purchased the outfits. He had not yet visited the yacht, but the man had given him the gate's entrance key for the place where the vessel was docked. So, Bruce was happy that all this was progressing so well.

The yacht was scheduled to depart in a specific month, and the client decided he should demonstrate patience. Then, that person suddenly had some events in his family, which prevented him from being available to Bruce through the phone. He traveled. He apologized. Bruce waited. Nothing happened. Bruce insisted. The contact was slipping.

Then, one day, Bruce took the key for the gate to the place where the yacht was docked and went there, deciding to have a definitive answer. When he put the key to the lock and turned it, the gate did not open. Bruce tried to find someone there who could bring him to the person in charge of the yacht. Finally, he found someone—who informed him that "the person in charge of the yacht" had never worked there and nobody knew that man.

Months later, telling this story to the author, Bruce was still despondent: "Why?! Why did he do this to me? I did not do anything bad to him! This was so mean, so cruel!" Of course, that person had exerted significant negative control over Bruce for a long time. The analyst observed to him, though, that on that specific day, he grabbed the key and went to the dock to check the liar, to exercise his inner authority, and found out what was going on—in an adult way.

Similar to how Bruce has conceived his marriage proposals, one could ponder how fascinated and excited he could be by extraordinary circumstances. He believed that these ideal situations could compensate for his certainty that he is not good enough. It is easy to seduce him with the outstanding—which sustains his narcissism and makes him unconscious so that he is naïve enough to "forget" to check on reality. He does not suspect the liar. But that day, he went to check, and this is certainly a positive step, although painful.

On the other hand, one could note the connection between Bruce's desired job on the yacht—a metaphor, of course—and the description of a boat presented by *The Book of Symbols. Reflections on Archetypal Images*:

> The boat immediately evokes a passage and the containing vessel that carries one over watery depth. The soundness of the boat is important because its integrity comprises a boundary, sometimes between life and death. For this reason, in most cultures, boat building has been surrounded by ritual practices, taboos, and superstitions that have to do with the tension between forces that function to keep the boat afloat and those that would submerge it. The basic form of any boat is the empty space it contains as well as the "cavity" it makes on the surface of the water; the boat's resiliency depends on this small incursion in the water's domain.[13]

That relationship between the vessel and the deep waters that buoy it up—and can also break it into pieces—is rhythmic and emotional. It brings back to us a link with our first crossing into birth, with the uterus, the rocking cradle, and the saving ark and with our last crossing in the ship of death "leading us back to the swaying gliding somnolent rhythms of earliest childhood, of the primordial ocean and the night." (See Erich Neumann, *The Great Mother*.)

For all these reasons, the ship—and, in Bruce's case, the desired yacht—has often been associated with aspects of the great feminine, as a mother or a beloved, whose holding body the captain or navigator must intimately know.

Friendship with the Gods as a Gambler

Since the initial therapy sessions, Bruce told the author that his father was a good chess player and a good poker player. He had taught the client how to play.

"It reminds me of my father—he would say—that's my thing. It takes time, you must be patient, but a chess game, for example, is good for your mind. I do not drink, don't do drugs, don't chase women—but if I know the right percentage and bet on that, at a casino, I can earn more than with Uber—where I make $15 per hour—and interact with people."

Indeed, Bruce could spend seven hours nonstop at a casino, and, taking into consideration what one could ponder about the archetype of the *puer*, we can clearly understand why he would feel at home there.

James Hillman, in his article "Puer Wounds and Ulysses' Scar," says:

> Perhaps, the *puer* spirit may not be meant to manage but to imagine. In the hands of a *puer* are shapes and gestures, and the *puer* touch, but not the reins of will. The desultory execution, the indecision that cannot grasp the sword hilt and slash a way forward may be symptomatic not only of what is wrong. It may also hint at something right: that one way forward is not via action but fantasy, *the way of imagination*. And fantasy is not wildly inspirational only. It has its laws and will, its intrinsic intelligibility of forms that the hands follow in each craft. The strict demands of a craft—those fantasies that will be crafted with precision into shapes—provide discipline and an ethic for an imaginal ego. By staying true to the *puer* archetype and its transcendent function, Buce worked at his crippling from within the imagination.[14]

Pondering the storylines considered in connection with this case, one could say that *fantasy* is Bruce's real job. That's the reason he feels empowered in a casino. In that place, instead of working hard in the real world, he can bet on his fantasy. He is allowed to trust his friendship with the Gods. If these powerful friends grant him a good bet, he wins. On top of that, he does not need to be scared to be trapped in something real. And he can be industrious: the ego and the libido are present when he is a gambler. He is allowed to be a trickster too—a gambler's facet—and play a part in many situations, although that's not stable.

The casino and what it offers Bruce are certainly extraordinarily more exciting—for a *puer*—than a tedious job as a driver or a salesman. And one could also remember that his father was a God to him: a war hero whose voice was like a lion roaring taught him how to play well, and carried, perhaps, the archetype of the *puer aeternus* himself.

In summary, within his emotionally alive therapeutic relationship, Bruce presented himself as a swift-footed boy, mimetic to a numinous Hermes, or an Icarus ascending too close to the sun, both personifications of a *puer.* In the beginning, the author felt as if he did not try to do anything hard or challenging. When, in their analytical process, they approached a territory closer to the ground, he would do his best to go away, to protect himself from the grief. His symptoms appeared to be expressions of his damaged ability to metaphorize past and present—processes that had been interrupted in their flow from the past to the present and from the present to the past. Bit by bit, though, as a metaphorical language adequate to create sounds and meanings that reflected what *it feels like* to think, feel, and physically experience a given moment, the polysemy that was lost in his neurotic suffering started to be restored.

From that perspective, one could say what was mentioned by Jeanine M. Vivona when she refers to poetry as a development into insight. She says:

> The experience of hearing a good poem or a good interpretation is of being understood and at the same time seeing something new about oneself that has been articulated by someone else from within that other person's own experience. The change that can happen in hearing such language we call *insight.* Insight is not only knowledge, not only content. It is an experience of resonance with another person's vision of things.[15]

That insight is the terrain where the poet, the Jungian analyst, the analysand, and the reader of this book find themselves together, hand in hand with the metaphor.

The Music of What Happens

In this chapter, one could have observed examples of *significant metaphors in the author's practice, which opened new dimensions to therapeutic work progress* with clients. She shared these examples from a point of view analogous to Thomas Ogden's when he talks about the relationship between the way he listens to the language of a poem and the way he and his patient speak with and listen to one another. Meaning that the analyst is not primarily engaged in an effort to unearth what lies "behind" or "beneath" the patient's report of a dream or a life event. Instead—as mentioned in chapter 7—Ogden attempts to listen to the sound and feel of what is going on, to'the music of what happens."[16] This is achieved to a significant degree in the analytic process by the analyst attending to his own reverie experience.

In fact, in the past fifty years, the analytical process has shifted, and the "What does this mean?" question has been expanded to "What's going on here?" In this chapter, one could have addressed that question in the following way: "What is happening between us consciously and unconsciously, and how does that relate to other aspects of the patient's (and the analyst's) past and present experience, both real and imagined?" That shift brings us to a necessary change in how we use language to speak to ourselves and to our patients—in an analogous way that we may process a poem, a metaphor.

NOTES

1. Rich, Adrienne. *Culture, Politics, and the Art of Poetry: Essential Essays* (New York: W. W. Norton & Co., 2018).
2. Rich, Adrienne. *Culture, Politics, and the Art of Poetry: Essential Essays* (New York: W. W. Norton & Co., 2018).
3. Clifton, L. "blessing the boats." *Blessing the Boats: New and Selected Poems 1988–2000* (Rochester, NY: BOA Editions Ltd., 2000).
4. Ogden, T. H. "Some Thoughts on the Use of Language in Psychoanalysis" (*Psychoanalytic Dialogues* 7, 1997): 1–21.
5. Ibid.
6. Ibid.
7. Basho. *The Complete Haiku of Matsuo Basho* (Los Angeles: University of California Press, 2022).
8. Edinger, E. *The Eternal Drama: The Inner Meaning of Greek Mythology* (Boston: Shambhala Publications, Inc., 1994), 83.
9. Clifton, L. "blessing the boats." *Blessing the Boats: New and Selected Poems 1988–2000* (Rochester, NY: BOA Editions Ltd., 2000).
10. Ibid.
11. Hillman, J. "Puer Wounds and Ulysses' Scar." *Puer Papers* (Dallas, TX: Spring Publications, Inc., 1987), 101.
12. Kast, Verena. *Imagination as Space of Freedom: Dialogue Between the Ego and the Unconscious* (New York: International Publishing Corporation, 1993), 15.
13. Ibid.
14. Hillman, J. "Puer Wounds and Ulysses' Scar." *Puer Papers* (Dallas, TX: Spring Publications, Inc., 1987), 101.
15. Vivona, J. M. "Embodied Language in Neuroscience and Psychoanalysis" (*J. Amer. Psychoanal. Assn.* 57, no. 6, 2009): 1327–60.
16. Ogden, T. H. "Some Thoughts on the Use of Language in Psychoanalysis" (*Psychoanalytic Dialogues* 7, 1997): 1–21.

Chapter 9

Concluding Comments

A noteworthy direction in the recent history of the analytical process has shown increased awareness by the analyst toward how effects created in language—meaning what the analysand's language *does* "alongside and beyond" what it *says*—brings essential contributions to the revelation of unconscious content. The study of metaphor constitutes a fundamental example of that direction.

The aim of this book has been (1) to demonstrate the vital intersection of poetry and the practice of Jungian analysis through the metaphor, (2) to contribute to an enriching language in the emotionally alive psychoanalytic process, (3) to validate that the mind functions metaphorically when faced with challenges requiring creativity, (4) to show that trauma leads to a degradation of metaphorical processes to mere repetitions of compulsion, (5) to observe that interpretation uses the metaphorical process in the analysand as well as in the analyst in order to restore the diminished metaphor capacity, and (6) to reveal that, because metaphor delivers a deep sensorimotor experience to the person's physical and emotional system, both metaphors encountered in the analysis as well as in a good poem empowers transformation.

In the author's experience, while she has been a cognitive neuroscientist, worked in two psychiatric hospitals, and in private practice, she is also a poet. She has been writing, studying, and publishing poetry for as long as her experience as a psychologist unfolds. Therefore, she has been learning and taking pleasure in how meaning is made and transformed in both areas: poetry and clinical work. One could consider that what we have been discussing in this book regarding the intersection of poetry and Jungian analysis practice through metaphor can be connected to a poem the author wrote, "Wild Beauty." *The Cortland Review* published that poem. As a conclusion, Regina Colonia-Willner would like to give the reader that poem.

Wild Beauty
You do not need to believe
each one of your thoughts.
Sometimes they slide
as Chagall lovers in the wind.
Yet wild
beauty teaches us.
Did you know that children
grow faster in spring?
That your bones
are twice as tough as granite?
That our left lung
is smaller than the right
because there needs to be room
for the heart?
You do not have to trust
the structure where you live
for its elements
— the roof, the science paper, the flags
fluttering out of your passport upstairs —
may embrace for a time in a place,
but none
might corral the newness of identity.
You can stand tall, though,
on the ground where giraffes feed
from the top of acacia trees
by the waterfall,
where we dance, therefore we are,
and we cry, therefore we change,
in the wild freedom
beyond grasping.

— Regina Colonia-Willner ©
Originally published in *The Cortland Review* of New York.

Bibliography

The Archive for Research in Archetypal Symbolism (ARAS). *The Book of Symbols: Reflections on Archetypal Images* (Cologne, Germany: Taschen, 2010).

Bass, E. "Conversation between Ellen Bass and Alan Fox" (*Rattle* #40, 2013): 1–7.

Bly, Robert. *Leaping Poetry* (Pittsburgh: University of Pittsburgh Press, 2008).

Borbely, A. "A Psychoanalytic Concept of Metaphor," (*International Journal of Psychoanalysis* 79, 1998): 923–36.

Bosselaar, L. A. "Stillbirth." *A New Hunger*. (Keene, NY: Ausable Press, 2007).

Brodersen, E. *Taboo, Personal and Collective Representations: Origin and Positioning within Cultural Complexes* (New York: Routledge, 2019).

Brown, K. "A Moment." *The Cortland Review,* 2014): 1.

Clayton, David. "Learning Birdsong by Imitation: Transforming Sensory Information into Vocal Imitation Allows Young Finches to Sing." (*Science* 366, no. 6461, 2019): 33.

Clifton, L. "Blessing the Boats." *Blessing the Boats: New and Selected Poems 1988–2000* (Rochester, NY: BOA Editions Ltd., 2000).

Daniel, Renate. *Taking the Fear out of the Night: Coping with Nightmares* (Einsiedeln, Switzerland: Daimon Verlag, 2016).

Dobyns, S. *Best Words, Best Order: Essays on Poetry* (New York: Palgrave Macmillan, 2003).

Dobyns, S. "Good Days." *The Day's Last Light Reddens the Leaves of the Copper Beech* (Rochester, NY: BOA Editions Ltd., 2016).

Dobyns, S. *Next Word, Better Word: The Craft of Writing Poetry* (New York: Palgrave Macmillan, 2011).

Edinger, E. *Anatomy of the Psyche* (La Salle, IL: Open Court Pub Co., 1985).

Edinger, Edward. *Ego and Archetype* (Boston: Shambhala Publications, 1972).

Edinger, E. *The Eternal Drama: The Inner Meaning of Greek Mythology* (Boston: Shamballa Publications, Inc., 1994).

Egger, Brigitte. The Symbol in Analytical Psychology: A Vivifying Experience, 2017.* "Oldest Dated Cave Art Points to Neandertal Symbolic Behavior." *Science Magazine* (Vol. 359, Number 6378, 2018), 852 and 912.

Eliade, Mircea. *Images and Symbols. Studies in Religious Symbolism* (Princeton, NJ: Princeton University Press, 1991).

Forché, C. "The Boatman." The Poetry Foundation, 2016.
Frey-Rohn, L. *From Freud to Jung. Comparative Study of the Psychology of the Unconscious* (Boston & Shaftesbury: Shambhala Publications, Inc., 1990).
Frost, R. "Acquainted with the Night." *Robert Frost: Collected Poems, Prose, and Plays* (New York: Library of America, 1995), 234.
Heaney, S. "Postscript." *Opened Ground: Selected Poems 1966–1996* (New York: Farrar, Straus and Giroux, 1998).
Hillman, J. "Puer Wounds and Ulysses' Scar." *Puer Papers* (Dallas, TX: Spring Publications, Inc., 1987), 101.
Hillman, J. *Re-Visioning Psychology* (New York: Harper & Row, 1975).
Hirshfield, Jane. "Autumn." *The Paris Review* 109.
Hirshfield, Jane. "Poetry, Permeability, and Healing." Academy of American Poets, 2023, 1–2.
Howe, M., and Nick Patrick. "Backchat: Marie Howe in Conversation." *American Poet* 54: 2018.
Jung, C. G. *Collected Works* (Princeton NJ: Princeton University Press, 1944).
Jung, C. G. *Collected Works* (Princeton, N. J.: Princeton University Press, 1969).
Jung, C. G. *Nietzsche's Zarathustra. Notes of the Seminar Given in 1934–1939* (Princeton, NJ: Princeton University Press, 1989).
Kast, Verena. *Imagination as Space of Freedom. Dialogue Between the Ego and the Unconscious* (New York: International Publishing Corporation, 1993).
Kast, V. *Joy, Inspiration, and Hope* (College StationX: Texas A&M University Press, 1991).
Kast, Verena, Mario Jacoby, and Ingrid Riedel. *Witches, Ogres, and the Devil's Daughter. Encounters with Evil in Fairy Tales* (Boston: Shambhala, 1992).
Leary, David (ed.), *Metaphors in the History of Psychology* (New York: Cambridge University Press, 1990).
Limón, A. "Naming the Animal." *The Writer's Chronicle*, 2019, 17.
Merwin, W. S. "The Art of Poetry." *The Paris Review* 38, no. 102, 1987.
Merwin, W. S. "For the Anniversary of My Death." *The Second Four Books of Poems* (Port Townsend, WA: Copper Canyon Press, 1992).
Nye, N. S. "Two Countries." *From Words Under the Words: Selected Poems* (New York: Far Corner, 1995).
Ogden, T. H. "The Music of What Happens in Poetry and Psychoanalysis" (*International Journal of Psychoanalysis* 80, 1999): 979–94.
Ogden, T. H. "Some Thoughts on the Use of Language in Psychoanalysis" (*Psychoanalytic Dialogues* 7, 1997): 1–21.
Oliver, Mary. *Devotions: The Selected Poems of Mary Oliver* (New York: Penguin Random House, 2017).
Phillips, Emilia. "Wislawa Szymborska's Influence on Poetry." *Ploughshares*, 2018.
Rich, Adrienne. *Culture, Politics, and the Art of Poetry: Essential Essays* (New York: W. W. Norton & Co., 2018).
Samuels, Andrew, Bani Shorter, and Fred Plaut. *A Critical Dictionary of Jungian Analysis* (New York: Routledge, 1987).

Seiden, Henry. *The Motive for Metaphor: Brief Essays on Poetry and Psychoanalysis* (New York: Routledge, 2018).

Slavin, Marc. *Metaphor and Imaginal Psychology: A Hermetic Reflection* (New York: Routledge, 2018).

Strand, M., and E. Boland eds. *The Making of a Poem: A Norton Anthology of Poetic Forms* (London: W.W. Norton & Company Ltd., 2001).

Sze, Arthur. "Sleepers." Academy of American Poets, 2019.

Szymborska, Wislawa, *New and Collected Poems.* Tr. S. Baranczak, S. and C. Cavanagh (New York: Harcourt, 1998).

Tillich, Paul. *Theology of Culture* (New York: Oxford University Press, 1964).

Ulanov, Ann, and Barry Ulanov. *Cinderella and Her Sisters: The Envied and the Envying* (Philadelphia: The Westminster Press, 1983).

Vivona, J. M. "Embodied Language in Neuroscience and Psychoanalysis" (*Journal of the American Psychological Association* 57(6), 2009): 1327–60.

Vivona, J. M. "Embracing Figures of Speech: The Transformative Potential of Spoken Language" (*Psychoanalytic Psychology* 20(1), 2003).

Vivona, J. M. "From Developmental Metaphor to Development Model: The Shrinking Role of Language in the Talking Cure" (*Journal of the American Psychoanalytic Association* 54, 2006): 894.

Vivona, J. M. "Psychoanalysis as Poetry" (*Journal of the American Psychoanalytic Association*, 2013): 1109–37.

Williams, W. C. "Asphodel. That Greeny Flower." *Pictures from Brueghel and Other Poems* (New York: New Directions, 1962), 153–82.

Winborn, M. "Interpretation in Jungian Analysis." (New York: *Art and Technique*, 2019), 21.

Winborn, Mark. *Working with Disruptions in Symbolic Capacity in Jungian Analysis: Theory and Practice* (Moscow, Russia: Moscow Association for Analytical Psychology Post Graduate Studies Program, 2019–2020).

Index

About the Author

Regina Célia Colonia-Willner is a licensed clinical psychologist. She holds a PhD in neuroscience from Georgia Institute of Technology, and received a degree from the Carl Gustav Jung Institut Zurich, where she defended her thesis "In Creation, You Are Created. The Intersection of Poetry and Jungian Analysis through the Metaphor." She is an accredited psychoanalyst at the Carl Gustav Jung Institut Zurich (CGJIZ) and a member of the International Association for Analytical Psychology (IAAP). She has received the George E. Briggs Dissertation Award and the Earl A. Alluisi Early Career Achievement Award from the American Psychological Association (APA). A fellow of APA, Colonia-Willner has served as an elected member of the APA Council for six years. Her peer-reviewed scientific papers have been published by APA, Elsevier, and *The International Journal of Behavioral Development* (ISSBD).

In the field of literature, Regina Célia Colonia is the author of four collections of poetry and short stories, including *Canção para o Totem* (Song for the Totem), which won the Jabuti Prize, Brazil's Pulitzer. Her poems have appeared in *Catamaran Literary Reader, The Cortland Review*, and elsewhere in the United States. Her fiction appears in the anthology *Urban Voices—Contemporary Short Stories from Brazil,* published by the University Press of America. Colonia-Willner is working on her new collection of poems, *Into the Blooming Night*. She is a preliminary reader at Tupelo Press.

Regina's books are published in Portuguese and French and anthologized in English, French, German, Italian, and Polish. Colonia's collection of poems *Sumaimana*, written in Portuguese was recently translated and published in France in a bilingual edition.

Regina Colonia-Willner was born in Rio de Janeiro, grew up in Paris, and lives in the United States. She has worked as a journalist and diplomat in several countries, serving in Brazil, Senegal, Portugal, and the United States. In addition, she has taught literature abroad, as in Budapest and Debrecen, Hungary. Regina has held the position of Writer-in-Residence at the University of Georgia. Her work as a writer has been supported by residences at the Colrain Conference in 2020 and 2021, the TWH Conference in 2021, and a Fellowship Award from Tupelo Press in 2022.

www.ingramcontent.com/pod-product-compliance
Lightning Source LLC
LaVergne TN
LVHW091532200926
848483LV00002B/372